The Spok

Tskhinvali: Sh

Edited by Ken Coates

Published by Spokesman for the Bertrand Russell Peace Foundation

Spokesman 101 **2009**

CONTENTS

Cover: A preliminary drawing for Guernica by Pablo Picasso.

Printed by the Russell Press Ltd., Nottingham, UK

SN 1367 7748

ISBN 978 0 85124 757 1

Subscriptions
Institutions £35.00
Individuals £20.00 (UK)
£25.00 (ex UK)

Back issues available on request

A CIP catalogue record for this book is available from the British Library

Published by the
Bertrand Russell Peace Foundation Ltd.,
Russell House
Bulwell Lane
Nottingham NG6 0BT
England
Tel. 0115 9784504
email:
elfeuro@compuserve.com
www.spokesmanbooks.com
www.russfound.org

Editorial

Tskhinvali: Shock and Awe

Georgia's war

On 7th August 2008, President Saakashvili of Georgia launched an all-out military assault on the capital town of South Ossetia, Tskhinvali. The town was partly destroyed. Estimates of civilian deaths vary, between fifteen hundred and two thousand. Precise figures may become available quite soon, now that it is possible to recover and bury the dead*. Thirty-four thousand South Ossetians fled to the neighbouring territory of North Ossetia, which is part of the Federal Russian State, and they can all talk. They have been doing so incessantly, telling stories of untrammelled brutality.

Tskhinvali was left without water, electricity or gas. The bombardment was continuous, not only from the air, but also by salvoes of Katyusha type rockets based in lethal batteries close to the Georgian town of Gori. When the children of Tskhinvali thought that it was safe to crawl out of the basements into the streets, looking for food, all too often they were shot by Georgian forces. These had also killed many Russian peacekeepers who had been based in the town under the Treaty that settled the previous civil war, which broke out with the collapse of the Soviet Union, and the subsequent abrogation of South Ossetian and other autonomies by the newly proclaimed Republic of Georgia.

On 21 August 1968, the armies of the Soviet Union and some of its allies in the Warsaw Treaty pushed into Czechoslovakia to terminate the Prague Spring, with its aspiration of 'socialism with a human face'. In London, the great Russian cellist, Mstislav Rostropovich, was scheduled to perform at a concert which excited some demonstrations on behalf of the Czechs. On the programme was the Cello Concerto by Dvorak. For many in the audience there was a profound symbolism in hearing this work performed at this time. They were wrung out by its passion. The maestro himself, while he played, was drenched in tears.

Forty years later, another musician, Valeri Gergiev, the Ossetian Principal Conductor of the London Symphony Orchestra, journeyed to the ruins of Tskhinvali after the invasion by Georgian troops, to give another concert. His programme included the Leningrad Symphony by Shostakovich, wrought from the traumas of the Nazi siege of that city. The tears this time were those of a whole people.

*On 28 August 2008, South Ossetia's Prosecutor General reported that 1,692 deaths resulted from Tbilisi's August offensive. 'We have information of 1,692 dead and 1,500 injured as a result of the Georgian aggression,' Russian Interfax news agency quoted Teimuraz Khugayev as saying.

The population of South Ossetia was mainly Russian speaking, and identified more strongly with Russia than with Georgia. It had been located within the Georgian Soviet Republic as a result of the 1936 Stalin constitution, which no doubt reflected the needs of the Soviet power at the time. Once the Soviet Union was destroyed, now that the successors of Mr. Beria were gone, South Ossetian residents had no reason to trust a purely Georgian Government, which was, for them, under permanent suspicion of ethnic hostility. They had promptly been told by Georgia's first President, Ghamsakhurdia, that there would be no more autonomy for minorities in the new Georgia. 'Georgia is for Georgians,' he proclaimed. When they (inevitably) rebelled, the Russian Government of President Yeltsin understood their predicament, and resolved to issue Russian passports to all those in the disputed areas who wished to have them. Russian pension entitlements were superior to anything available locally, so that many older people would be influenced in their choice of nationality. Estimates vary, but it seems likely that by 2008 some ninety-five per cent of the inhabitants of the area had opted to hold Russian passports, rejecting Georgian ones. After Saakashvili's barbaric onslaught this August, the near unanimity of the South Ossetian public is assured.

The short war that was waged with such total ruthlessness was also brought to a paroxysm in the Western media, which bought all the lies dispensed by Mr. Saakashvili's propaganda machine as if they were the very milk of the gospel. Whilst the killing and burning was raging, the news media in the West found it impossible to be in any way specific about who was killing whom, who was applying the torch. Normal viewers of the TV channels were very likely to form the impression that it was the Russians who were responsible for all that destruction, all those deaths. A

> The Kingdom of Georgia was shaped in the early eleventh century from the Kingdom of Iberia (which had adopted Christianity in the fourth century) and the Kingdom of Colchis, land of the Golden Fleece, which drew the Argonauts to the east of the Black Sea. Georgia thrived for a couple of centuries before fragmenting into various principalities and lesser kingdoms in the sixteenth century. Three centuries of Ottoman or Persian hegemony followed before piecemeal absorption in the Russian Empire. During that time Georgia had no independent existence. Briefly independent as a Menshevik republic from 1918 to 1921, during which it suffered British occupation of Batumi, and the incursion of various White armies, it was incorporated into the Russian Soviet Federative Socialist Republic in 1921. After the collapse of the Soviet Union, it became an independent republic.

veritable wave of hysteria was launched, in which, for a short time, the real culprits succeeded in offsetting their responsibilities, laying all blame at the feet of their victims.

In the beginning, undoubtedly, the Georgian propaganda machine was in control of its lies. It was very effective, and its numerous friends in the Western media did their duty. But with the arrival of the Russian army to support their beleaguered citizens and murdered peacekeepers, everything rapidly changed. Firstly, there were Russian news media, widely suspect in the West, but, given a strong case, bound to penetrate the fog of what were clearly blatant lies. But secondly, the Georgian army did not expect to stand up to a proper army, one that might fire back, and after a brief indecision, it ran away. Indeed, it surpassed the Olympic runners. As it ran, the force of rumour became a tidal wave.

Meantime, the other contested province, Abkhazia, had seized the opportunity to drive out Georgian forces that had previously occupied the Kodori Gorge. So the Georgian army was in flight from several directions. As it ran, the news travelled that the Russians were coming. Perhaps the Russians were not coming. But the Georgians were certainly going. When they reached the town of Gori there were ferocious disputes about who would snaffle which vehicles. To whom would go the fastest cars? In fevered flight from non-existent Russians, all headed for the capital, Tbilisi. There they were advertised as the phantom Russians. It seems likely now that at least some of the deserting soldiers have taken off their uniforms and melted into the landscape. After all that excitement, the Russians did arrive. Their first action was to restrain Ossetian irregulars who had gone on the rampage, and seek to restore the civil authority of Gori's mayor.

Of course, part of the American trained Georgian army had been deployed in Iraq, where it comprised the third largest contingent of the occupation forces. The Americans obligingly flew them straight back to Georgia so that they could do their duty in defending Tbilisi and Mr. Saakashvili's regime. We do not know whether they got home in time to join their invasion, or whether they arrived a little later, during the rout. In either case, it cannot be excluded that they will join the backlash of Georgian opinion, which will probably hold their President responsible for a disastrous military adventure.

Saakashvili's helpers

But this disaster did not occur for want of careful preparation. For several years the Georgian Government had been energetically preparing for a war, lavishing millions on various kinds of weaponry, with the highest average growth rate of military expenditure in the whole world, according to the Stockholm International Peace Research Institute. From $18 million in 2002, this rose to $900 million in 2008. This was accompanied by a prodigious diplomatic effort to build what they hoped would be military support. The support of the neo-cons in the United States was buttressed by the provision of a pro-Georgian lobby which placed one of its people in a close advisory role to Presidential candidate John McCain. His top foreign policy adviser, the neo-con Randy Scheunemann, is said to have had a long-term financial relationship with President Saakashvili, as a lobbyist for his American interests. According to the *Wall Street Journal*:

> 'In 2005, Mr. Scheunemann asked Senator McCain to introduce a Senate resolution expressing support for peace in the Russian-influenced region of South Ossetia that wants to break away from Georgia, the records show.
>
> Such resolutions of Senate support are symbolic but helpful to countries in their diplomatic relations. The Senate approved Senator McCain's resolution in December 2005, and the Georgian Embassy posted the text on its Website.
>
> Senator McCain has endorsed Georgia's goal of entering Nato, a matter for which the country hired Mr. Scheunemann to lobby. In 2006, Senator McCain gave a speech at the Munich Conference on Security in Germany in which he said "Georgia has implemented far-reaching political, economic, and military reforms" and should enter Nato, a text of his speech on the conference Website shows.'

Writing in *The Nation*, Mark Ames reported:

> 'Scheunemann … also worked for recently-disgraced Bush fundraiser Stephen Payne, lobbying for his Caspian Alliance oil business. The Caspian oil pipeline runs through Georgia, the main reason that country has tugged the heartstrings of neo-cons and oil plutocrats for at least a decade or more.
>
> In 2006, McCain visited Georgia and denounced the South Ossetian separatists, proving that Scheunemann wasn't wasting his Georgian sponsor's money. At a speech he gave in a Georgian army base in Senaki, McCain declared that Georgia was America's "best friend", and that Russian peacekeepers should be thrown out.'

There was another best friend. The Israelis established a private company called Defensive Shield, run by Gal Hirsch, previously a General in the Israeli army. This obtained a contract to train Georgian troops. Gal Hirsch arouses a particular interest in the Lebanon, where the leader of Hezbollah, Hassan Nasrallah, has kept a close eye on his progress since his downfall after the abortive Israeli onslaught on the Lebanon in 2006. Nasrallah might be forgiven a modest gloat when the Georgian armed forces came a similar cropper in 2008. 'Israel exported failed generals in order to train the Georgian armed forces', he said, comparing their victorious progress into and out of the Lebanon with that of their Georgian apprentices into and out of South Ossetia.

But the true story of Israeli involvement seems to be quite complicated. Misha Glenny maintains that:

> 'The Russians … knew all about Defensive Shield and the tens of millions of dollars worth of Israeli military equipment that Georgia had been purchasing. Just over a week before the conflict erupted Putin put in a call to the Israeli President, Shimon Peres. His message, according to a Western intelligence source, was simple: pull out your trainers and weapons or we will escalate our co-operation with Syria and Iran.'

Glenny says that Peres does not suffer from the same illusions as Georgia's Ministers, 'and the Israeli set-up left Tbilisi within two days'.

But President Saakashvili denied on Wednesday 13th August that Israel had suspended its aid to the country. 'I have not heard anything about that', he told *Haaretz*. Saakashvili said that he was aware of difficulties with the supply of pilotless drones that had been ordered by his army, but not of the stopping of any other shipments of military aid. 'The Israeli weapons have proved very effective', he said. A reporter asked him about the Jews who had fled the fighting and gone to Israel. Saakashvili replied:

> 'We have two Israeli cabinet ministers, one deals with war, Defence Minister David Kezerashvili, and the other with negotiations, State Minister for Territorial Integration, Temur Yakobashvili, and that is the Israeli involvement here: both war and peace are in the hands of Israeli Jews.'

According to *Haaretz*, Yakobashvili is not actually an Israeli citizen.

> 'Saakashvili's statements are part of his Government's attempt to bring other countries into its war against Russia. During the briefing, he noted that he is in constant contact with US Vice President Dick Cheney and Secretary of State Condoleezza Rice.'

Be all that as it may, none of it stopped the Russians from capturing very large numbers of Israeli weapons. They also seem to have impounded considerable stocks from Ukraine, to say nothing of those that had been provided by the Americans. There has been some speculation about what the Russians will do with these mountains of weaponry which have fallen into their hands, and which, it was said, they might destroy, or take back into South Ossetia. One Russian officer demurred from these proposals. We shall send them back home, he said, so that we can use them where they remain useful.

Thus, in short order, ended years of intensive preparations by President Saakashvili. Perhaps he will set off again to climb the same mountain: but his survival cannot be guaranteed, since it seems at least possible that the

Georgian people may tire of these dreams of military grandeur.

It being difficult for the Americans to find another expeditionary force to throw into the Georgian fray, diplomatic weapons have been chosen. Mrs. Merkel has been suborned into promising that Georgia can join Nato. But Georgia might seem a modest liability with no weapons, not much army left, and two festering military defeats. All these might well constitute an inoculation against the military contagion.

There hasn't been much the Americans could do about all this. True, President Bush decided to send a contingent of American troops to Georgia on Wednesday 14th August. The American military were to carry out a humanitarian mission. A C-17 transporter, said to be carrying medical supplies and tents for thousands of people displaced by the fighting, was the first American plane to arrive in Tbilisi from Germany. The second flight was due to arrive the following day.

Condoleezza Rice announced that she was going to visit Georgia after calling off in Paris for a meeting with President Sarkozy. She told Foreign Minister Lavrov on the telephone about the relief operation and said that the presence of American troops would not only help the aid mission, but also allow the Americans to monitor how far the Russians were honouring the ceasefire. Ms. Rice then called a news conference of considerable belligerence, telling the Russians that this was not 1968, when Russia could 'invade its neighbour, occupy a capital, overthrow a government and get away with it'. Apparently nowadays only America can do that. But the fact remains that the Russian Government is quite different from the Soviet Government of 1968, even if the Americans are seeking to persuade it to revert to type.

It is too early to say what is the meaning of this American humanitarian surge. Do they simply want to give tents to the victims of their proxy, who now find themselves homeless? Or are they looking for ways to provoke unpleasant reactions from their former 'partners' in Russia? All this rhetoric, whatever it means, has not gone unremarked in Moscow. Mr. Lavrov said: 'We understand that this current Georgian leadership is a special project of the United States. But one day the United States will have to chose between defending its prestige over a virtual project or a real partnership', with Russia.

What consequences?

But the Americans have speeded up their confrontational responses in other areas, starting in Poland with the installation of a missile interceptor programme, and some new Patriot missiles. The Russians have never been under any doubt about where all these will be trained, and nobody believes that this programme has been installed to defend against non-existent Iranian missiles. Of course, if the confrontation between East and West continues, and continues to escalate, it is not inconceivable that the Iranians might be able to obtain appropriate missiles. But why they should want to do so has never been explained. Iran would prove incredibly vulnerable in a nuclear confrontation, and is likely to be wide open to the proposal for agreements about nuclear-free zones for a long time to come. But nobody in the West wants to make such sensible proposals. They do not suit Israel.

However, Iran might take some small comfort from the possibility that the Nato allies might come to revise their commercial relations with Iranian energy suppliers in the light of these heavy military engagements. The same thing applies to those Nato forces which are deployed in Afghanistan. Not so long ago, they concluded a deal on the transit of non-lethal cargo through Russian territory to their forces deployed in Afghanistan. The deal mainly concerned food and non-military supplies, but did include some kinds of military equipment. The supplies were to be transported across Russia, Kazakhstan and Uzbekistan.

The Hindu reported on the 26th June 2008 that:

> 'Two decades after it pulled out of Afghanistan, Russia is returning, at the request of the United States and the North Atlantic Treaty Organisation. Moscow will allow land shipment of Nato supplies to Afghanistan across the Russian territory and will supply weapons to the Afghan army.
>
> There is a rich irony in the fact that the US, which fought a proxy war against the Russian forces in Afghanistan from 1979-1989, is now asking Russia to help Nato combat the same mujahideen who were armed and trained by Washington to fight the Russians.
>
> Russia promised to resume defence supplies to Afghanistan at a meeting of the Russia-US Working Group on Counterterrorism in Moscow last week. This will greatly boost Nato efforts to rearm the Afghan army and enable it to stand up to the Taliban. Russian weapons make up almost 100 per cent of Afghan inventory, and are far more popular with local combatants than western arms.'

Over seventy per cent of all Nato supplies to Afghanistan go through Pakistan with the rest flown in by air. The route has recently proved extremely hazardous with the Taliban stepping up attacks on the US and Nato convoys. 'The Russian corridor will greatly reduce Nato dependence on the violence-plagued Pakistani route.'

No one in Nato knows for sure what will be the effect of the resignation of President Musharraf on the Pakistani supply routes. So it might be thought a hazardous engagement to place the newly agreed Russian route in jeopardy. But when he visited Germany in May 2008, Russia's new

President Medvedev said that Nato should not jeopardise co-operation with Russia in Afghanistan by clinging to the inertia of bloc mentality. In Bucharest, at the April Nato summit, Mr. Putin said that the alliance could not achieve anything in Afghanistan without Russian help:

> 'Is it possible to succeed in Afghanistan without Russia, given its vast capabilities in the region? Negative. That is why we are being constantly urged to open transit, provide aid, etc.'

Meantime, the nuclear dimension to all this continues to be aggravated. Indeed, its shadow has already fallen across Georgia: press secretary Dana Perino and Ambassador Jeffrey reported on Sunday 10th August 2008 that President Bush had been immediately informed 'when we received news of the first two SS-21 Russian missile launchers (in) Georgian territory'. These launchers are capable of carrying warheads which are conventional, but it is not, from the military point of view, an optimal use to make of them. They are, of course, designed to carry nuclear warheads. The Americans did not have to spell this out to President Bush:

> 'He immediately – this was at the Great Hall – he immediately met with President Putin. They had a discussion. The President then engaged with his national security staff continuously over the last two days. He has spoken with – again with Putin that evening. He then talked with President Medvedev yesterday evening, as well as President Saakashvili. Secretary Rice has spoken repeatedly with President Saakashvili, as well as with her Russian counterpart, Foreign Minister Lavrov, and many European leaders.'

Subsequently, President Bush announced that there would be no American military intervention. Were the SS-21s a symbolic warning to the Americans? Were they intended to show that the Russians were serious, and meant business? Or were they real? Bush, universally derided as an impulsive hothead, wisely decided not to confront this matter further.

But immediately there followed the announcement about Polish deployment of an anti-missile system, and immediately thereafter, a flurry of lesser diplomats and presidents went to Tbilisi to announce the impending welcome of Georgia into Nato.

For their part, the Russians have not hesitated to escalate the nuclear deployments. There has been public speculation about fitting nuclear warheads to the missiles carried by the Baltic fleet. There has also been sustained discussion of the deployment of nuclear warheads in Kaliningrad, formerly Königsberg, the Russian outpost at the entrance to the Baltic Sea. None of this may happen, but all of it might.

The ghost at this lunatic banquet, however, is not in all these endangered territories. It is the giant threat of Ukraine, already a participant in the arming of Georgia, and a collaborator of President Saakashvili. President Yushchenko has already required the Russian fleet to report its movements in advance to their homeports, including Sevastopol, and they have already declared their lack of readiness to oblige. But of course, the outstanding applications for membership of Nato came both from Georgia and Ukraine. Perhaps there are some who doubt the significance of this. If Ukraine were to join Nato the minnow of Georgia would be replaced by a whale. If nuclear confrontation were to continue to escalate, would anyone be sure that we were not standing on the very brink of the Third World War? Can Russia possibly accept such a move? And Russia may not need to accept it, because although only one-third or less of the Ukrainian population are ethnic Russians, a vast proportion of the Ukrainian Orthodox population is closer to Russia economically and culturally than they are to Catholic Western Ukraine, and if that country were to break in two, as appears possible, then the anti-Russian part of the country may have no visible means of support.

Already this prospect has been borne in on Ukrainian leaders, so that we learn that President Yushchenko is seeking to explore how he might lay treason charges against fellow orange revolutionary, Prime Minister Yulia Tymoshenko. Apparently she is alarmed by the virulence of Yushchenko's espousal of the Georgian cause, and has refused to allow the Ukrainian Parliament to adopt an anti-Russian stance or to condone the eviction of the Russian fleet from Ukrainian waters. She also declined to join an official delegation to Tbilisi on August 9th. Why? Well, clearly she understands that Ukraine is heading for a split which could either result in a reassertion of Russian hegemony, or a division of the country.

When one examines the paroxysms of threats and demagogic blustering that have attended Saakashvili's wars in Georgia, one is perhaps alerted to the very much worse consequences of an attempt to plant Nato in Kiev.

Ken Coates

With thanks to Tony Benn, Nigel Harris, Bruce Kent, Henry McCubbin, Zhores Medvedev, Jan Oberg and Tony Simpson

Georgia and nuclear warfare

Col. Sam Gardiner, retired US Air Force Colonel, has taught strategy and military operations at the National War College, Air War College and Naval War College. He was interviewed by Amy Goodman on Democracy Now! Radio in the United States on 11 August 2008, from which this excerpt is taken.

Amy Goodman: Can you talk about significance of this, in terms of nuclear warfare in Russia? Do we have anything to fear along those lines?

Col. Sam Gardiner: Absolutely. Let me just say that if you were to rate how serious the strategic situations have been in the past few years, this would be above Iraq, this would be above Afghanistan, and this would be above Iran.

On little notice to Americans, the Russians learned at the end of the first Gulf War that they couldn't – they didn't think they could deal with the United States, given the value and the quality of American precision conventional weapons. The Russians put into their doctrine a statement, and have broadcast it very loudly, that if the United States were to use precision conventional weapons against Russian troops, the Russians would be forced to respond with tactical nuclear weapons. They continue to state this. They practise this in their exercise. They've even had exercises that very closely paralleled what went on in Ossetia, where there was an independence movement, they intervene conventionally to put down the independence movement, the United States and NATO responds with conventional air strikes, they then respond with tactical nuclear weapons.

It appears to me as if the Russians were preparing themselves to do that in this case. First of all, I think they believe the United States was going to intervene. At a news conference on Sunday, the deputy national security adviser said we have noted that the Russians have introduced two SS-21 medium-range ballistic missile launchers into South Ossetia. Now, let me say a little footnote about those. They're both conventional and nuclear. They have a relatively small conventional warhead, however. So, the military significance, if they were to be conventional, was almost trivial compared to what the Russians could deliver with the aircraft that they were using to strike the Georgians.

I think this was a signal. I think this was an implementation on their part of their doctrine. It clearly appears as if they expected the United States to do what they had practised in their exercises. In fact, this morning, the Russians had an air defence exercise in the southern part of Russia that borders Georgia in which they – it was practising shooting down incursion aircraft that were incursion into Russia. They were prepared for the United States to intervene, and I think they were prepared – or at least they were wanting to show the United States that their doctrine of the use of tactical nuclear weapons, if the US attacks, was serious, and they needed to take – the United States needs to take Russia very seriously.

America's role in Georgia?

Vladimir Putin

Russian Prime Minister Vladimir Putin was interviewed by CNN's Matthew Chance in Sochi on 28 August 2008. CNN broadcast part of the interview, from which this transcript of the translation is taken.

Putin: … At this time it was in Bejing and I had an opportunity to have a brief discussion with the President of the United States. George told me that no one wants a war. I hoped that the US Administration would intervene to stop the aggression of the Georgian leadership, but nothing of this kind happened.

CNN: You've always enjoyed over your period as President of Russia, and still now, a very close personal relationship with the US President, George W. Bush. Do you think his failure to restrain the Georgian forces on this occasion has damaged that relationship?

Putin: Of course it has damaged our relations, first and foremost inter-state relations. But the thing is that not only has the US Administration failed to restrain the leadership from committing this criminal act, but in fact it equipped and trained the Georgian army.

But I have some other comments to add. Even during the Cold War, during the time of tough confrontation between the Soviet Union and the US, we have always avoided direct clashes between our civilians, let alone our servicemen. We have serious reasons to believe that directly in the combat zone citizens of the United States were present, and if this is the case then the suspicion arises that someone in the United States has, on purpose, created this conflict with a view to exacerbating the situation and creating a competitive advantage for one of the Presidential candidates in the United States.

CNN: These are quite astounding claims. Just to be clear, Mr Prime Minister, are you suggesting there were US operatives on the ground assisting Georgian forces perhaps in provoking a conflict in order to give a Presidential candidate in the United States some kind of talking point? And if you are suggesting that, what evidence do you have?

Putin: I've told you that if the facts are confirmed that American citizens were present in the combat zone, that means only one thing, that they could be there only on the direct instruction of their leadership. And if this is so, then it means that American citizens are in the combat zone performing their duties and they can only do that following a direct order from their leaders and not on their own initiative. Ordinary experts, even if they are providing training in military matters, should do that not in a combat zone but at training ranges and training centres. I repeat this needs to be checked out further. I'm telling you this based on what our military told me.

In Praise of the High Shadow

Mahmoud Darwish

In memory of Mahmoud Darwish, Palestine's most eminent poet, who died on 9 August 2008. Saifedean Ammous of The Electronic Intifada *writes.*

For me, the most memorable of Darwish's work will always remain his seminal poem, 'Madeeh al-Thill al-'Aaly' (In Praise of the High Shadow). The poem was written on the deck of one of the ships carrying Darwish, along with thousands of Palestinian fighters, from Beirut to Tunisia after Israel's barbaric destruction of Lebanon in 1982. Darwish recounts the daily realities of living under shelling and under siege in Beirut, the deafening silence of the rest of the world towards the plight of the Palestinians and Lebanese, and the harrowing details of the Sabra and Shatila massacre. Acerbic, witty and powerful, Darwish skewers everyone from the Israeli government murdering civilians while pretending to be the victim ('You stole our tears, wolf'), to the American government ('The Plague') giving every child a cluster bomb toy as a gift, to the Arab governments ('the bastard nations').

Yet through it all, and as dark as the plight becomes, Darwish never loses sight of the humanism at the heart of his cause and at the heart of the Palestinian struggle. He continuously disparages nationalism and mocks its silliness. The ending of the poem, in particular, serves as a sort of Palestinian anti-Zionist humanist manifesto. In it, Darwish addresses the Palestinian fighter with powerful rhetorical questions, asking him about the true nature of his cause, and what he is really after. Mocking the trappings of nationalism and statehood, Darwish – in no uncertain terms – asserts that the cause has always been about humans, about freedom from oppression, about the revolution against persecution, about the ideals of liberty, and not about nationalism and the toys of statehood.

In Praise of the High Shadow

It is for you to be, or not to be,
It is for you to create, or not to create.
All existential questions, behind your shadow, are a farce,
And the universe is your small notebook, and you are its creator.
So write in it the paradise of genesis,
Or do not write it,
You, you are the question.
What do you want?
As you march from a legend, to a legend?
A flag?
What good have flags ever done?
Have they ever protected a city from the shrapnel of a bomb?
What do you want?
A newspaper?
Would the papers ever hatch a bird, or weave a grain?
What do you want?
Police?
Do the police know where the small earth will get impregnated from the coming winds?
What do you want?
Sovereignty over ashes?
While you are the master of our soul; the master of our ever-changing existence?
So leave,
For the place is not yours, nor are the garbage thrones.
You are the freedom of creation,
You are the creator of the roads,
And you are the anti-thesis of this era.
And leave,
Poor, like a prayer,
Barefoot, like a river in the path of rocks,
And delayed, like a clove.

You, you are the question.
So leave to yourself,
For you are larger than people's countries,
Larger than the space of the guillotine.
So leave to yourself,

Resigned to the wisdom of your heart,
Shrugging off the big cities, and the drawn sky,
And building an earth under your hand's palm – a tent, an idea, or a grain.
So head to Golgotha,
And climb with me,
To return to the homeless soul its beginning.
What do you want?
For you are the master of our soul,
The master of our ever-changing existence.
You are the master of the ember,
The master of the flame.
How large the revolution,
How narrow the journey,
How grand the idea,
How small the state!

An excerpt from the poem by Mahmoud Darwish
Translated by Saifedean Ammous
www.electronicintifada.net

New American Cold War

Stephen F Cohen

We reprint this article as a timely commentary on the United States' deteriorating relations with Russia over an extended period, which have now been highlighted in responses to the war in the Caucasus. It first appeared in The Nation *in the United States in July 2006, and the author added a new introduction a year later.*

Stephen F. Cohen, Professor of Russian studies at New York University, is the author (with Katrina vanden Heuvel) of Voices of Glasnost: Conversations With Gorbachev's Reformers *and, most recently,* Failed Crusade: America and the Tragedy of Post-Communist Russia *(both Norton).*

Two reactions to this article were particularly noteworthy when it first appeared in 2006. Judging by activity on *The Nation's* website and by responses sent to me personally, it was very widely read and discussed both in the United States and in Russia, where it was quickly translated on a Russian-language site. And, unlike most Russian commentators, almost every American specialist who reacted to the article, directly or indirectly, adamantly disputed my thesis that US-Russian relations had deteriorated so badly they should now be understood as a new Cold War – or possibly as a continuation of the old one.

Developments during the last year have amply confirmed that thesis. Several examples could be cited, but two should be enough. The increasingly belligerent charges and counter-charges by officials and in the media on both sides, 'Cold-War-style rhetoric and threats', as the Associated Prcss recently reported, read like a replay of the American-Soviet discourse of the 1970s and early 1980s. And the unfolding conflict over US plans to build missile defence components near post-Soviet Russia, in Poland and the Czech Republic, threatens to reintroduce a dangerous military feature of that Cold War era in Europe.

None the less, most American officials, journalists and academics, unwilling perhaps to confront their unwise policies and mistaken analyses since the Soviet Union ended in 1991, continue to deny the Cold War nature of today's relationship with Russia. A resident expert at the Council on Foreign Relations tells us, for example, that 'the situation today is nothing like the Cold War times', while another think-tank specialist, testifying to Congress, can 'see no prospect of a new Cold War'.

Indeed, many commentators even insist that Cold War is no longer possible because today's US-Russian conflicts are not global, ideological or clashes between two different systems; because post-Soviet Russia is too weak to wage such a struggle; and because of the avowed personal 'friendship' between Presidents Bush and Putin. They seem unaware that the last Cold War began regionally, in Central and Eastern Europe; that present-day antagonisms between Washington's 'democracy-promotion' policies and Moscow's self-described 'sovereign democracy' have become intensely ideological; that Russia's new, non-Communist system is scarcely like the American one; that Russia is well situated, as I explained in the article, to compete in a new Cold War whose front lines run through the former Soviet territories, from Ukraine and Georgia to Central Asia; and that there was also, back in the Cold-War 1970s, a Nixon-Brezhnev 'friendship'.

Nor is this merely an academic dispute. Unless US policy-makers and opinion-makers recognize how bad the relationship has become, we risk losing not only the historic opportunity for an American-Russian partnership created in the late 1980s by Gorbachev, Reagan and the first President Bush, and which is even more essential for our real national security today; we also risk a prolonged Cold War even more dangerous than was the last one, for reasons spelled out in my article.

Still worse, the overwhelming majority of US officials and opinion-makers who do acknowledge the serious deterioration in relations between Washington and Moscow blame the development solely on Putin's domestic and foreign policies. Not surprisingly, the most heretical part of my article – that the origins of the new Cold War are to be found instead in attitudes and policies toward post-Soviet Russia adopted by the Clinton administration back in the 1990s and largely continued by this Bush administration – has found even less support. But unless it, too, is fully acknowledged, we are left only with the astonishing admission of a leading academic specialist with longstanding ties in Washington. Lamenting the state of US-Russian relations, he informs us, 'Nobody has a good idea of what is to be done'.

What must be done, however, is clear enough. Because the new Cold War began in Washington, steps toward ending it also have to begin in Washington. Two are especially urgent, for reasons also explained in the article: a US recognition that post-Soviet Russia is not a defeated supplicant or American client state, as seems to have been the prevailing view since 1991, but a fully sovereign nation at home with legitimate national interests abroad equal to our own; and an immediate end to the reckless expansion of Nato around Russia's borders.

According to principles of American democracy, the best time to fight for such a change in policy is in the course of campaigns for the presidency. That is why I am pleased my article is reappearing at this time. On the other hand, the hour is late, and it is hard to be optimistic.

Stephen F. Cohen
8 June 2007

* * *

Contrary to established opinion, the gravest threats to America's national security are still in Russia. They derive from an unprecedented development that most US policy-makers have recklessly disregarded, as evidenced by the undeclared Cold War Washington has waged, under both parties, against post-Communist Russia during the past fifteen years.

As a result of the Soviet break-up in 1991, Russia, a state bearing every nuclear and other device of mass destruction, virtually collapsed. During the 1990s its essential infrastructures – political, economic and social – disintegrated. Moscow's hold on its vast territories was weakened by separatism, official corruption and Mafia-like crime. The worst peacetime depression in modern history brought economic losses more than twice those suffered in World War Two. Gross domestic product plummeted by nearly half and capital investment by 80 per cent. Most Russians were thrown into poverty. Death rates soared and the population shrank. And, in August 1998, the financial system imploded.

No one in authority anywhere had ever foreseen that one of the twentieth century's two superpowers would plunge, along with its arsenals of destruction, into such catastrophic circumstances. Even today, we cannot be sure what Russia's collapse might mean for the rest of the world.

Outwardly, the nation may now seem to have recovered. Its economy has grown on average by six to seven per cent annually since 1999, its stock-market index increased last year by 83 per cent, and its gold and foreign currency reserves are the world's fifth largest. Moscow is booming with new construction, frenzied consumption of Western luxury goods, and fifty-six large casinos. Some of this wealth has trickled down to the provinces and middle and lower classes, whose income has been rising. But these advances, loudly touted by the Russian government and Western investment-fund promoters, are due largely to high world prices for the country's oil and gas and stand out only in comparison with the wasteland of 1998.

More fundamental realities indicate that Russia remains in an unprecedented state of peacetime demodernization and depopulation. Investment in the economy and other basic infrastructures remains barely a third of the 1990 level. Some two-thirds of Russians still live below or very near the poverty line, including 80 per cent of families with two or more children, 60 per cent of rural citizens and large segments of the educated and professional classes, among them teachers, doctors and military officers. The gap between the poor and the rich, Russian experts tell us, is becoming 'explosive'.

Most tragic and telling, the nation continues to suffer wartime death and birth rates, its population declining by 700,000 or more every year. Male life expectancy is barely 59 years and, at the other end of the life cycle, two to three million children are homeless. Old and new diseases, from tuberculosis to HIV infections, have grown into epidemics. Nationalists may exaggerate in charging that 'the Motherland is dying', but even the head of Moscow's most pro-Western university warns that Russia remains in 'extremely deep crisis'.

The stability of the political regime atop this bleak post-Soviet landscape rests heavily, if not entirely, on the personal popularity and authority of one man, President Vladimir Putin, who admits the state 'is not yet completely stable'. While Putin's ratings are an extraordinary 70 to 75 per cent positive, political institutions and would-be leaders below him have almost no public support.

The top business and administrative élites, having rapaciously 'privatized' the Soviet state's richest assets in the 1990s, are particularly despised. Indeed, their possession of that property, because it lacks popular legitimacy, remains a time bomb embedded in the political and economic system. The huge military is equally unstable, its ranks torn by a lack of funds, abuses of authority and discontent. No wonder serious analysts worry that one or more sudden developments – a sharp fall in world oil prices, more major episodes of ethnic violence or terrorism, or Putin's disappearance – might plunge Russia into an even worse crisis. Pointing to the disorder spreading from Chechnya through the country's southern rim, for example, the eminent scholar Peter Reddaway even asks 'whether Russia is stable enough to hold together'.

As long as catastrophic possibilities exist in that nation, so do the unprecedented threats to US and international security. Experts differ as to which danger is the gravest – proliferation of Russia's enormous stockpile of nuclear, chemical and biological materials; ill-maintained nuclear reactors on land and on decommissioned submarines; an impaired early-warning system controlling missiles on hair-trigger alert; or the first-ever civil war in a shattered superpower, the terror-ridden Chechen conflict. But no one should doubt that together they constitute a much greater constant threat than any the United States faced during the Soviet era.

Nor is a catastrophe involving weapons of mass destruction the only danger in what remains the world's largest territorial country. Nearly a quarter of the planet's people live on Russia's borders, among them conflicting ethnic and religious groups. Any instability in Russia could easily spread to a crucial and exceedingly volatile part of the world.

There is another, perhaps more likely, possibility. Petrodollars may bring Russia long-term stability, but on the basis of growing authoritarianism and xenophobic nationalism. Those ominous factors derive primarily not from Russia's lost superpower status (or Putin's KGB background), as the US press regularly misinforms readers, but from so many lost and damaged lives at home since 1991. Often called the 'Weimar scenario', this outcome probably would not be truly fascist, but it would be a Russia possessing weapons of mass destruction and large proportions of the world's oil and natural gas, even more hostile to the West than was its Soviet predecessor.

How has the US government responded to these unprecedented perils? It doesn't require a degree in international relations or media punditry to understand that the first principle of policy toward post-Communist Russia must follow the Hippocratic injunction: do no harm! Do nothing to undermine its fragile stability, nothing to dissuade the Kremlin from giving first priority to repairing the nation's crumbling infrastructures, nothing to cause it to rely more heavily on its stockpiles of superpower weapons instead of reducing them, nothing to make Moscow uncooperative with the West in those joint pursuits. Everything else in that savaged country is of far less consequence.

Since the early 1990s Washington has simultaneously conducted, under Democrats and Republicans, two fundamentally different policies toward post-Soviet Russia – one decorative and outwardly reassuring, the other real and exceedingly reckless. The decorative policy, which has been taken at face value in the United States, at least until recently, professes to have replaced America's previous Cold War intentions with a generous relationship of 'strategic partnership and friendship'. The public image of this approach has featured happy-talk meetings between American and Russian Presidents, first 'Bill and Boris' (Clinton and Yeltsin), then 'George and Vladimir'.

The real US policy has been very different – a relentless, winner-take-all exploitation of Russia's post-1991 weakness. Accompanied by broken American promises, condescending lectures and demands for unilateral concessions, it has been even more aggressive and uncompromising than was Washington's approach to Soviet Communist Russia. Consider its defining elements as they have unfolded – with fulsome support in both American political parties, influential newspapers and policy think tanks – since the early 1990s:

- A growing military encirclement of Russia, on and near its borders, by US and Nato bases, which are already ensconced or being planned in at least half the fourteen other former Soviet republics, from the Baltics and Ukraine to Georgia, Azerbaijan and the new states of Central Asia. The result is a US-built reverse iron curtain and the remilitarization of American-Russian relations.
- A tacit (and closely related) US denial that Russia has any legitimate national interests outside its own territory, even in ethnically akin or contiguous former republics such as Ukraine, Belarus and Georgia. How else to explain, to take a bellwether example, the thinking of Richard Holbrooke, Democratic would-be Secretary of State? While roundly condemning the Kremlin for promoting a pro-Moscow government in neighbouring Ukraine, where Russia has centuries of shared linguistic, marital, religious, economic and security ties, Holbrooke declares that far-away Slav nation part of 'our core zone of security'.
- Even more, a presumption that Russia does not have full sovereignty within its own borders, as expressed by constant US interventions in Moscow's internal affairs since 1992. They have included an on-site crusade by swarms of American 'advisers', particularly during the 1990s, to direct Russia's 'transition' from Communism; endless missionary sermons from afar, often couched in threats, on how that nation should and should not organize its political and economic systems; and active support for Russian anti-Kremlin groups, some associated with hated Yeltsin-era oligarchs.
- That interventionary impulse has now grown even into suggestions that Putin be overthrown by the kind of US-backed 'colour revolutions' carried out since 2003 in Georgia, Ukraine and Kyrgyzstan, and attempted in 2006 in Belarus. Thus, while mainstream editorial pages increasingly call the Russian president 'thug', 'fascist' and 'Saddam Hussein', one of the Carnegie Endowment's several Washington crusaders assures us of 'Putin's weakness' and vulnerability to 'regime change'. (Do proponents of 'democratic regime change' in Russia care that it might mean destabilizing a nuclear state?)

- Underpinning these components of the real US policy are familiar Cold War double standards condemning Moscow for doing what Washington does – such as seeking allies and military bases in former Soviet republics, using its assets (oil and gas in Russia's case) as aid to friendly governments, and regulating foreign money in its political life. More broadly, when NATO expands to Russia's front and back doorsteps, gobbling up former Soviet-bloc members and republics, it is 'fighting terrorism' and 'protecting new states'; when Moscow protests, it is engaging in 'Cold War thinking'. When Washington meddles in the politics of Georgia and Ukraine, it is 'promoting democracy'; when the Kremlin does so, it is 'neo-imperialism'. And not to forget the historical background: when in the 1990s the US-supported Yeltsin overthrew Russia's elected Parliament and Constitutional Court by force, gave its national wealth and television networks to Kremlin insiders, imposed a constitution without real constraints on executive power and rigged elections, it was 'democratic reform'; when Putin continues that process, it is 'authoritarianism'.
- Finally, the United States is attempting, by exploiting Russia's weakness, to acquire the nuclear superiority it could not achieve during the Soviet era. That is the essential meaning of two major steps taken by the Bush Administration in 2002, both against Moscow's strong wishes. One was the Administration's unilateral withdrawal from the 1972 Anti-Ballistic Missile Treaty, freeing it to try to create a system capable of destroying incoming missiles and thereby thc capacity to launch a nuclear first strike without fear of retaliation. The other was pressuring the Kremlin to sign an ultimately empty nuclear weapons reduction agreement requiring no actual destruction of weapons and indeed allowing development of new ones; providing for no verification; and permitting unilateral withdrawal before the specified reductions are required.

The extraordinarily anti-Russian nature of these policies casts serious doubt on two American official and media axioms: that the recent 'chill' in US-Russian relations has been caused by Putin's behaviour at home and abroad, and that the Cold War ended fifteen years ago. The first axiom is false, the second only half true: the Cold War ended in Moscow, but not in Washington, as is clear from a brief look back.

The last Soviet leader, Mikhail Gorbachev, came to power in 1985 with heretical 'New Thinking' that proposed not merely to ease but to actually abolish the decades-long Cold War. His proposals triggered a fateful struggle in Washington (and Moscow) between policy-makers who wanted to seize the historic opportunity and those who did not. President Ronald Reagan decided to meet Gorbachev at least part of the way, as did his successor, the first President George Bush. As a result, in December 1989, at a historic summit meeting at Malta, Gorbachev and Bush declared the Cold War over. (That extraordinary agreement evidently has been forgotten; thus we have the *New York Times* recently asserting that the US-Russian relationship today 'is far better than it was 15 years ago'.)

Declarations alone, however, could not terminate decades of warfare attitudes. Even when Bush was agreeing to end the Cold War in 1989-91, many of his top advisers, like many members of the US political élite and media, strongly resisted. (I witnessed that rift on the eve of Malta, when I was asked to debate the issue in front of Bush and his divided foreign policy team.) Proof came with the Soviet break-up in December 1991: US officials and the media immediately presented the purported 'end of the Cold War' not as a mutual Soviet-American decision, which it certainly was, but as a great American victory and Russian defeat.

That (now standard) triumphalist narrative is the primary reason the Cold War was quickly revived – not in Moscow a decade later by Putin, but in Washington in the early 1990s, when the Clinton Administration made two epically unwise decisions. One was to treat post-Communist Russia as a defeated nation that was expected to replicate America's domestic practices and bow to its foreign policies. It required, behind the facade of the Clinton-Yeltsin 'partnership and friendship' (as Clinton's top 'Russia hand', Strobe Talbott, later confirmed), telling Yeltsin 'here's some more shit for your face', and Moscow's 'submissiveness'. From that triumphalism grew the still-ongoing interventions in Moscow's internal affairs and the abiding notion that Russia has no autonomous rights at home or abroad.

Clinton's other unwise decision was to break the Bush Administration's promise to Soviet Russia in 1990-91 not to expand Nato 'one inch to the east' and instead begin its expansion to Russia's borders. From that profound act of bad faith, followed by others, came the dangerously provocative military encirclement of Russia and growing Russian suspicions of US intentions. Thus, while American journalists and even scholars insist that 'the Cold War has indeed vanished' and that concerns about a new one are 'silly', Russians across the political spectrum now believe that in Washington 'the Cold War did not end' and, still more, that 'the US is imposing a new Cold War on Russia'.

That ominous view is being greatly exacerbated by Washington's ever-growing 'anti-Russian fatwa', as a former Reagan appointee terms it. In

2006 it included a torrent of official and media statements denouncing Russia's domestic and foreign policies, vowing to bring more of its neighbours into Nato and urging Bush to boycott the G-8 summit to be chaired by Putin in St. Petersburg in July that year; a call by Republican presidential nominee Senator John McCain for 'very harsh' measures against Moscow; Congress's pointed refusal to repeal a Soviet-era restriction on trade with Russia; the Pentagon's revival of old rumours that Russian intelligence gave Saddam Hussein information endangering US troops; and comments by Secretary of State Condoleezza Rice, echoing the regime-changers, urging Russians, 'if necessary, to change their government'.

For its part, the White House deleted from its 2006 National Security Strategy the long-professed US-Russian partnership, backtracked on agreements to help Moscow join the World Trade Organization, and adopted sanctions against Belarus, the Slav former republic most culturally akin to Russia and with whom the Kremlin is negotiating a new union state. Most significant, in May 2006 it dispatched Vice President Cheney to an anti-Russian conference in former Soviet Lithuania, now a Nato member, to denounce the Kremlin and make clear it is not 'a strategic partner and a trusted friend', thereby ending fifteen years of official pretence.

More astonishing is a Council on Foreign Relations 'task force report' on Russia, co-chaired by Democratic Presidential aspirant John Edwards, issued in March. The 'non-partisan' Council's reputed moderation and balance are nowhere in evidence. An unrelenting exercise in double standards, the report blames all the 'disappointments' in US-Russian relations solely on 'Russia's wrong direction' under Putin – from meddling in the former Soviet republics and backing Iran to conflicts over Nato, energy politics and the 'rollback of Russian democracy'.

Strongly implying that Bush has been too soft on Putin, the Council report flatly rejects partnership with Moscow as 'not a realistic prospect'. It calls instead for 'selective cooperation' and 'selective opposition', depending on which suits US interests, and, in effect, Soviet-era containment. Urging more Western intervention in Moscow's political affairs, the report even reserves for Washington the right to reject Russia's future elections and leaders as 'illegitimate'. An article in the Council's influential journal *Foreign Affairs* menacingly adds that the United States is quickly 'attaining nuclear primacy' and the ability 'to destroy the long-range nuclear arsenals of Russia or China with a first strike'.

Every consequence of this bipartisan American Cold War against post-

Communist Russia has exacerbated the dangers inherent in the Soviet break-up mentioned above. The crusade to transform Russia during the 1990s, with its disastrous 'shock therapy' economic measures and resulting antidemocratic acts, further destabilized the country, fostering an oligarchical system that plundered the state's wealth, deprived essential infrastructures of investment, impoverished the people, and nurtured dangerous corruption. In the process, it discredited Western-style reform, generated mass anti-Americanism where there had been almost none – only 5 per cent of Russians surveyed in May 2006 thought the United States was a 'friend' – and eviscerated the once-influential pro-American faction in Kremlin and electoral politics.

Military encirclement, the Bush Administration's striving for nuclear supremacy and today's renewed US intrusions into Russian politics are having even worse consequences. They have provoked the Kremlin into undertaking its own conventional and nuclear build-up, relying more rather than less on compromised mechanisms of control and maintenance, while continuing to invest miserly sums in the country's decaying economic base and human resources. The same American policies have also caused Moscow to co-operate less rather than more in existing US-funded programmes to reduce the multiple risks represented by Russia's materials of mass destruction and to prevent accidental nuclear war. More generally, they have inspired a new Kremlin ideology of 'emphasizing our sovereignty' that is increasingly nationalistic, intolerant of foreign-funded non-governmental organisations as 'fifth columns', and reliant on anti-Western views of the 'patriotic' Russian intelligentsia and the Orthodox Church.

Moscow's responses abroad have also been the opposite of what Washington policy-makers should want. Interpreting US-backed 'colour revolutions' as a quest for military outposts on Russia's borders, the Kremlin now opposes pro-democracy movements in former Soviet republics more than ever, while supporting the most authoritarian regimes in the region, from Belarus to Uzbekistan. Meanwhile, Moscow is forming a political, economic and military 'strategic partnership' with China, lending support to Iran and other anti-American governments in the Middle East, and already putting surface-to-air missiles back in Belarus, in effect Russia's western border with Nato.

If American policy and Russia's predictable countermeasures continue to develop into a full-scale Cold War, several new factors could make it even more dangerous than was its predecessor. Above all, the growing presence of Western bases and US-backed governments in the former

Soviet republics has moved the 'front lines' of the conflict, in the alarmed words of a Moscow newspaper, from Germany to Russia's 'near abroad'. As a 'hostile ring tightens around the Motherland', in the view of former Prime Minister Evgeny Primakov, many different Russians see a mortal threat. Putin's chief political deputy, Vladislav Surkov, for example, sees the 'enemy … at the gates', and the novelist and Soviet-era dissident Aleksandr Solzhenitsyn sees the 'complete encirclement of Russia and then the loss of its sovereignty'. The risks of direct military conflict could therefore be greater than ever. Protesting overflights by Nato aircraft, a Russian general has already warned, 'If they violate our borders, they should be shot down'.

Worsening the geopolitical factor are radically different American and Russian self-perceptions. By the mid-1960s the US-Soviet Cold War relationship had acquired a significant degree of stability because the two superpowers, perceiving a stalemate, began to settle for political and military 'parity'. Today, however, the United States, the self-proclaimed 'only superpower', has a far more expansive view of its international entitlements and possibilities. Moscow, on the other hand, feels weaker and more vulnerable than it did before 1991. And in that asymmetry lies the potential for a less predictable Cold War relationship between the two still fully armed nuclear states.

There is also a new psychological factor. Because the unfolding Cold War is undeclared, it is already laden with feelings of betrayal and mistrust on both sides. Having welcomed Putin as Yeltsin's chosen successor and offered him its conception of 'partnership and friendship', Washington now feels deceived by Putin's policies. According to two characteristic commentaries in the *Washington Post*, Bush had a 'well-intentioned Russian policy', but 'a Russian autocrat … betrayed the American's faith'. Putin's Kremlin, however, has been reacting largely to a decade of broken US promises and Yeltsin's boozy compliance. Thus Putin's declaration four years ago, paraphrased on Russian radio: 'The era of Russian geopolitical concessions [is] coming to an end'. (Looking back, he remarked bitterly that Russia has been 'constantly deceived'.)

Still worse, the emerging Cold War lacks the substantive negotiations and co-operation, known as détente, that constrained the previous one. Behind the lingering facade, a well-informed Russian tells us, 'dialogue is almost non-existent'. It is especially true in regard to nuclear weapons. The Bush Administration's abandonment of the Anti-Ballistic Missile Treaty and real reductions, its decision to build an anti-missile shield, and talk of pre-emptive war and nuclear strikes have all but abolished long-established US-Soviet agreements that have kept the nuclear peace for nearly fifty years. Indeed, according to a report, Bush's National Security Council is contemptuous of arms control as 'baggage from the Cold War'. In short, as dangers posed by nuclear weapons have grown, and a new arms race unfolds, efforts to curtail or even discuss them have ended.

Finally, anti-Cold War forces that once played an important role in the United States no longer exist. Cold War lobbies, old and new ones, therefore operate virtually unopposed, some of them funded by anti-Kremlin Russian oligarchs in exile. At high political levels, the new American Cold War has been, and remains, fully bipartisan, from Clinton to Bush, Madeleine Albright to Rice, Edwards to McCain. At lower levels, once robust pro-détente public groups, particularly anti-arms-race movements, have been largely demobilized by official, media and academic myths that 'the Cold War is over' and we have been 'liberated' from nuclear and other dangers in Russia.

Also absent (or silent) are the kinds of American scholars who protested Cold War excesses in the past. Meanwhile, a legion of new intellectual cold warriors has emerged, particularly in Washington, media favourites whose crusading anti-Putin zeal goes largely unchallenged. (Typically, one inveterate missionary constantly charges Moscow with 'not delivering' on US interests, while another now calls for a surreal crusade, 'backed by international donors', to correct young Russians' thinking about Stalin.) There are a few notable exceptions – also bipartisan, from former Reaganites to *Nation* contributors – but 'anathematizing Russia', as Gorbachev recently put it, is so consensual that even an outspoken critic of US policy inexplicably ends an article, 'Of course, Russia has been largely to blame'.

Making these political factors worse has been the 'pluralist' US mainstream media. In the past, opinion page editors and television producers regularly solicited voices to challenge Cold War zealots, but today such dissenters, and thus the vigorous public debate of the past, are almost entirely missing. Instead, influential editorial pages are dominated by resurgent Cold War orthodoxies, led by the *Washington Post*, whose incessant demonization of Putin's 'autocracy' and 'crude neo-imperialism' reads like a bygone *Pravda* on the Potomac. On the conservative *New York Sun*'s front page, US-Russian relations today are presented as 'a duel to the death – perhaps literally'.

The Kremlin's strong preference 'not to return to the Cold War era', as Putin stated on 13 May 2006 in response to Cheney's inflammatory charges, has been mainly responsible for preventing such fantasies from becoming reality. 'Someone is still fighting the Cold War', a British academic recently wrote, 'but it isn't Russia'. A fateful struggle over this issue, however, is now under way in Moscow, with the 'pro-Western' Putin resisting demands for a 'more hard line' course and, closely related, favouring larger FDR-style investments in the people (and the country's stability). Unless US policy, which is abetting the hard-liners in that struggle, changes fundamentally, the symbiotic axis between American and Russian cold warriors that drove the last conflict will re-emerge. If so, the Kremlin, whether under Putin or a successor, will fight the new one – with all the unprecedented dangers that would entail.

Given different principles and determined leadership, it is still not too late for a new US policy toward post-Soviet Russia. Its components would include full co-operation in securing Moscow's materials of mass destruction; radically reducing nuclear weapons on both sides while banning the development of new ones, and taking all warheads off hair-trigger alert; dissuading other states from acquiring those weapons; countering terrorist activities and drug-trafficking near Russia; and augmenting energy supplies to the West.

None of those programmes are possible without abandoning the warped priorities and fallacies that have shaped US policy since 1991. National security requires identifying and pursuing essential priorities, but US policy-makers have done neither consistently. The only truly vital American interest in Russia today is preventing its stockpiles of mass destruction from endangering the world, whether through Russia's destabilization or hostility to the West.

All of the dangerous fallacies underlying US policy are expressions of unbridled triumphalism. The decision to treat post-Soviet Russia as a vanquished nation, analogous to post-war Germany and Japan (but without the funding), squandered a historic opportunity for a real partnership and established the bipartisan premise that Moscow's 'direction' at home and abroad should be determined by the United States. Applied to a country with Russia's size and long history as a world power, and that had not been militarily defeated, the premise was inherently self-defeating and certain to provoke a resentful backlash.

That folly produced two others. One was the assumption that the United States had the right, wisdom and power to remake post-Communist Russia into a political and economic replica of America. A conceit as vast as its ignorance of Russia's historical traditions and contemporary realities, it led to the counterproductive crusade of the 1990s, which continues in various ways today. The other was the presumption that Russia should be

America's junior partner in foreign policy with no interests except those of the United States. By disregarding Russia's history, different geopolitical realities and vital interests, this presumption has also been senseless.

As a Eurasian state with 20-25 million Muslim citizens of its own and with Iran one of its few neighbours not being recruited by Nato, for example, Russia can ill afford to be drawn into Washington's expanding conflict with the Islamic world, whether in Iran or Iraq. Similarly, by demanding that Moscow vacate its traditional political and military positions in former Soviet republics so the United States and Nato can occupy them – and even subsidize Ukraine's defection with cheap gas – Washington is saying that Russia not only has no Monroe Doctrine-like rights in its own neighbourhood but no legitimate security rights at all. Not surprisingly, such flagrant double standards have convinced the Kremlin that Washington has become more belligerent since Yeltsin's departure simply 'because Russian policy has become more pro-Russian'.

Nor was American triumphalism a fleeting reaction to 1991. A decade later, the tragedy of September 11 gave Washington a second chance for a real partnership with Russia. At a meeting on 16 June 2001, President Bush sensed in Putin's 'soul' a partner for America. And so it seemed after September 11, when Putin's Kremlin did more than any Nato government to assist the US war effort in Afghanistan, giving it valuable intelligence, a Moscow-trained Afghan combat force and easy access to crucial air bases in former Soviet Central Asia.

The Kremlin understandably believed that in return Washington would give it an equitable relationship. Instead, it got US withdrawal from the Anti-Ballistic Missile Treaty, Washington's claim to permanent bases in Central Asia (as well as Georgia), and independent access to Caspian oil and gas, a second round of Nato expansion taking in several former Soviet republics and bloc members, and a still-growing indictment of its domestic and foreign conduct. Astonishingly, not even September 11 was enough to end Washington's winner-take-all principles.

Why have Democratic and Republican administrations believed they could act in such relentlessly anti-Russian ways without endangering US national security? The answer is another fallacy – the belief that Russia, diminished and weakened by its loss of the Soviet Union, had no choice but to bend to America's will. Even apart from the continued presence of Soviet-era weapons in Russia, it was a grave misconception. Because of its extraordinary material and human attributes, Russia, as its intellectuals say, has always been 'destined to be a great power'. This was still true after 1991.

Even before world energy prices refilled its coffers, the Kremlin had ready alternatives to the humiliating role scripted by Washington. Above all, Russia could forge strategic alliances with eager anti-US and non-Nato governments in the East and elsewhere, becoming an arsenal of conventional weapons and nuclear knowledge for states from China and India to Iran and Venezuela. Moscow has already begun that turning away from the West, and it could move much further in that direction.

Still more, even today's diminished Russia can fight, perhaps win, a Cold War on its new front lines across the vast former Soviet territories. It has the advantages of geographic proximity, essential markets, energy pipelines and corporate ownership, along with kinship and language and common experiences. They give Moscow an array of soft and hard power to use, if it chooses, against neighbouring governments considering a new patron in faraway Washington.

Economically, the Kremlin could cripple nearly destitute Georgia and Moldova by banning their products and otherwise unemployed migrant workers from Russia and by charging Georgia and Ukraine full 'free-market' prices for essential energy. Politically, Moscow could truncate tiny Georgia and Moldova, and big Ukraine, by welcoming their large, pro-Russian territories into the Russian Federation or supporting their demands for independent statehood (as the West has been doing for Kosovo and Montenegro in Serbia). Militarily, Moscow could take further steps toward turning the Shanghai Cooperation Organization – composed of Russia, China and four Central Asian states, with Iran and India possible members – into an anti-Nato defensive alliance, an 'OPEC with nuclear weapons', a Western analyst warned.

That is not all. In the US-Russian struggle in Central Asia over Caspian oil and gas, Washington, as even the triumphalist Thomas Friedman admits, 'is at a severe disadvantage'. The United States has already lost its military base in Uzbekistan and may soon lose the only remaining one in the region, in Kyrgyzstan; the new pipeline it backed to bypass Russia runs through Georgia, whose stability depends considerably on Moscow; Washington's new friend in oil-rich Azerbaijan is an anachronistic dynastic ruler; and Kazakhstan, whose enormous energy reserves make it a particular US target, has its own large Russian population and is moving back toward Moscow.

Nor is the Kremlin powerless in direct dealings with the West. It can mount more than enough warheads to defeat any missile shield and illusion of 'nuclear primacy'. It can shut US businesses out of multibillion-dollar deals in Russia and, as it recently reminded the European Union, which gets 25 per cent of its gas from Russia, 'redirect supplies' to hungry markets in the East. And Moscow could deploy its resources, connections and UN Security Council veto against US interests involving, for instance, nuclear proliferation, Iran, Afghanistan and possibly even Iraq.

Contrary to exaggerated US accusations, the Kremlin has not yet resorted to such retaliatory measures in any significant way. But unless Washington stops abasing and encroaching on Russia, there is no 'sovereign' reason why it should not do so. Certainly, nothing Moscow has gotten from Washington since 1992, a Western security specialist emphasizes, 'compensates for the geopolitical harm the United States is doing to Russia'.

American crusaders insist it is worth the risk in order to democratize Russia and other former Soviet republics. In reality, their campaigns since 1992 have only discredited that cause in Russia. Praising the despised Yeltsin and endorsing other unpopular figures as Russia's 'democrats', while denouncing the popular Putin, has associated democracy with the social pain, chaos and humiliation of the 1990s. Ostracizing Belarus President Aleksandr Lukashenko while embracing tyrants in Azerbaijan and Kazakhstan has related it to the thirst for oil. Linking 'democratic revolutions' in Ukraine and Georgia to Nato membership has equated them with US expansionism. Focusing on the victimization of billionaire Mikhail Khodorkhovsky and not on Russian poverty or ongoing mass protests against social injustices has suggested democracy is only for oligarchs. And by insisting on their indispensable role, US crusaders have all but said (wrongly) that Russians are incapable of democracy or resisting abuses of power on their own.

The result is dark Russian suspicions of American intentions ignored by US policy-makers and media alike. They include the belief that Washington's real purpose is to take control of the country's energy resources and nuclear weapons and use encircling Nato satellite states to 'de-sovereignize' Russia, turning it into a 'vassal of the West'. More generally, US policy has fostered the belief that the American Cold War was never really aimed at Soviet Communism but always at Russia, a suspicion given credence by *Post* and *Times* columnists who characterize Russia even after Communism as an inherently 'autocratic state' with 'brutish instincts'.

To overcome those towering obstacles to a new relationship, Washington has to abandon the triumphalist conceits primarily responsible for the revived Cold War and its growing dangers. It means respecting Russia's sovereign right to determine its course at home (including disposal of its energy resources). As the record plainly shows, interfering in Moscow's internal affairs, whether on-site or from afar, only harms the chances for political liberties and economic prosperity that still exist in that tormented nation.

It also means acknowledging Russia's legitimate security interests, especially in its own 'near abroad'. In particular, the planned third expansion of Nato, intended to include Ukraine, must not take place. Extending Nato to Russia's doorsteps has already brought relations near the breaking point (without actually benefiting any nation's security); absorbing Ukraine, which Moscow regards as essential to its Slavic identity and its military defence, may be the point of no return, as even pro-US Russians anxiously warn. Nor would it be democratic, since nearly two-thirds of Ukrainians are opposed. The explosive possibilities were adumbrated in late May and early June 2006 when local citizens in ethnic Russian Crimea blockaded a port and roads where a US naval ship and contingent of Marines suddenly appeared, provoking resolutions declaring the region 'anti-Nato territory' and threats of 'a new Vietnam'.

Time for a new US policy is running out, but there is no hint of one in official or unofficial circles. Denouncing the Kremlin in May 2006, Cheney spoke 'like a triumphant cold warrior', a *New York Times* correspondent reported. A top State Department official has already announced the 'next great mission' in and around Russia. In the same unreconstructed spirit, Rice has demanded Russians 'recognize that we have legitimate interests … in their neighbourhood,' without a word about Moscow's interests; and a former Clinton official has held the Kremlin 'accountable for the ominous security threats … developing between Nato's eastern border and Russia'. Meanwhile, the Bush Administration is playing Russian roulette with Moscow's control of its nuclear weapons. Its missile shield project having already provoked a destabilizing Russian build-up, the Administration now proposes to further confuse Moscow's early-warning system, risking an accidental launch, by putting conventional warheads on long-range missiles for the first time.

In a democracy we might expect alternative policy proposals from would-be leaders. But there are none in either party, only demands for a more anti-Russian course, or silence. We should not be surprised. Acquiescence in Bush's monstrous war in Iraq has amply demonstrated the political élite's limited capacity for introspection, independent thought and civic courage. (It prefers to falsely blame the American people, as the managing editor of *Foreign Affairs* recently did, for craving 'ideological red meat'.) It may also be intimidated by another revived Cold War practice – personal defamation. The *Post* and *The New Yorker* have already labelled critics of their Russia policy 'Putin apologists' and charged them with 'appeasement' and 'again taking the Russian side of the Cold War'.

The vision and courage of heresy will therefore be needed to escape today's new Cold War orthodoxies and dangers, but it is hard to imagine a US politician answering the call. There is, however, a not-too-distant precedent. Twenty years ago, when the world faced exceedingly grave Cold War perils, Gorbachev unexpectedly emerged from the orthodox and repressive Soviet political class to offer a heretical way out. Is there an American leader today ready to retrieve that missed opportunity?

With grateful acknowledgements to The Nation (www.thenation.com)

Intelligence Disgrace

Andrew Mackinlay MP

On 22 May 2008, the Labour MP for Thurrock criticised the lack of accountability of the British intelligence organisations MI5 and MI6 when he spoke in the House of Commons.

There is never a right time to bring up the matter about which I want to detain the House. I am somewhat nervous about doing so. All too often, Members from all parties acquiesce by their silence in a slow undoing of our human rights and civil liberties in this country. We are not sufficiently zealous in fulfilling our role of probing those areas that the establishment in this country would not like us to dwell on. I am referring particularly … to our security and intelligence services.

I think that it is a thundering disgrace and an abdication of our responsibility in this House that there is no parliamentary oversight at all of the security and intelligence services. That is a severe deficiency and a flaw in our democratic institutions. Most of the great democracies have parliamentary committees charged with probing and overseeing their security and intelligence services, but that system does not exist here.

I have challenged successive Ministers about the matter, including the current Prime Minister. They have dismissed my questions by referring to the Intelligence and Security Committee, which is hand-picked by the Prime Minister of the day from parliamentarians with whom he or she – and, more importantly, the security and intelligence services – feels comfortable. One Minister told me, 'Mackinlay, this is a distinction without a difference,' but I disagree. Who clerks the Intelligence and Security Committee? It is clerked by a spook, a member of the security and intelligence services, and not by the Clerk of the House of Commons. When does it meet? We do not know. We do not know the parameters of its jurisdiction, as the term 'security and intelligence services' is a generic one: does it include the special branch of the Metropolitan Police and other forces, or does it involve just MI5, MI6 and GCHQ? We do not know.

That is a serious abdication on our part, and it is time that it was remedied – with some expedition, as Whips are already coming to me to talk about this business of the 42 days [detention without charge]. I have told them – I shall paint it on their eyelids – that there is no way that I am going to support that proposal. There are many reasons for that, but a particular one is the fact that there is no parliamentary oversight of our security and intelligence services.

Mr. Richard Bacon (South Norfolk) (Con): … will he acknowledge that there is some parliamentary oversight of the security and intelligence services, albeit not enough? Under the National Audit Act 1983, the Chairman of the Public Accounts Committee – who, by convention, is a member of the Opposition – has certain statutory responsibilities for auditing them.

Andrew Mackinlay: I am grateful to hear it. I do not mean to be disrespectful as I think that that is good, but it is barely a fig leaf. I make no apologies for saying that this place is abdicating its responsibilities, at a time when civil liberties are at stake – and, as I intend to go on to share with the House, when the role of this place is being undermined.

Dr. Julian Lewis (New Forest, East) (Con): … This House is a democratic Chamber, and all sorts of people get elected to it. Among its hundreds and hundreds of Members over many years, there might have been some who were genuinely a subversive danger. Does he accept that there must be some form of screening of the members of any parliamentary committee that has oversight of secret organisations and access to information that properly is held to be secret? Otherwise, the secret organisations will not make secret information available – and they shall be right not to do so.

Andrew Mackinlay: The answer to the hon. Gentleman is yes, I do accept that, but it is not the issue. The issue is that successive Labour and Tory Prime Ministers have said that there shall not be any parliamentary oversight, and I believe that they have done so because they are weak and craven before the security and intelligence services. The point that the hon. Gentleman raises is addressed in the US Congress, which has a very powerful committee to oversee security and intelligence matters. It does not appoint suspect people, but the pride of Congress – and of this place – is that parliamentary institutions should be able to make judgments of that sort.

… The fact is that the US Congress, France's National Assembly, Canada's House of Commons and Australia's House of Representatives all address this subject: it is a matter of pride for them. They find ways to ensure that the members of their respective committees are suitable and appropriate, but they are appointed not by the head of the security and intelligence services – that is, by each country's equivalent of the Prime Minister or the head of the CIA – but by their Parliament or Congress.

… I was going to save the story that I am about to tell for my memoirs. They will be the mother and father of all memoirs, and will actually be interesting. When the late Robin Cook was Foreign Secretary, he had to instruct a man called C to meet the Foreign Affairs Committee. I did not know that there really was a guy called C; I thought that such things were confined to films, but there really is one. I remember going down to the MI6 building, and the Committee was made as welcome as people with bubonic plague. It was clear that the then incumbent C deeply resented the fact that the Foreign Secretary had instructed him to see the Foreign Affairs Committee. Frankly, the meeting was not very productive, as the House can imagine …

Mr. Nigel Evans (Ribble Valley) (Con): … He has intimated that other Parliaments seem to get around the problem without threatening security. Will he be a little more constructive and suggest how we might change the custom by which the Prime Minister makes appointments to the Intelligence and Security Committee?

Andrew Mackinlay: … First of all, it should be a parliamentary committee. No doubt, there would always be discussions through the usual channels about the method and modus by which people are selected … but appointments to the committee would be a matter for Parliament. I think that people would emerge about whose qualifications all parties were confident. Achieving the sort of committee that I have described really is not rocket science.

Importantly – and this is not merely a shibboleth of mine – the committee's secretariat should be provided by the Clerk of the House of Commons. At present, as the House knows, the Clerk does handle confidential papers. Without going into too much detail, there are occasions when, rightly, items that require some discretion and security have to be held in this building. Therefore, that is not a problem.

The problem is that there is a cosy consensus among the people who run our political parties. I will not sign up to it, but they are craven before the security and intelligence services. No one is allowed to ask any questions at all, and I shall give an illustration of that very serious problem in a moment. I dismiss the idea that it cannot be resolved, and think that we should pursue it.

As I noted earlier, the parameters of what comes under the generic term 'security and intelligence services' are not quite clear. I want to emphasise that I have no doubt that some very dedicated and brave men and women work in those services, as I do not want anything that I might go on to say to be used against me. I will not accept any suggestion that I do not acknowledge the professionalism, bravery and patriotic dedication of the people who work for our security and intelligence services. However, what I do question is the arrogance of the culture surrounding those services that leads them to believe that they should be exempted from any oversight whatsoever of anything that they do, even when that stuff is almost a matter of history.

Soon after we return from the recess, the question of the 42 days will come before the House, but for me it is a matter of trust. Far too many things lately have caused me to reflect about whether I can trust what are described as the security and intelligence services. I regret that, but in any event it is certainly the mood of the very many people in our society who are asking the same question.

I will give one illustration to buttress my argument. I am one of the Members of Parliament who joined in a court case – Lord Alton of Liverpool and others *v.* the Secretary of State for the Home Department – and my interest in this matter is registered. It went to the Proscribed Organisations Appeals Commission – the POAC is of the status of the High Court – which found against the Home Secretary. In that judgment, it said the Home Secretary's action in relation to what is known as the People's Mujahedeen Organisation of Iran was perverse. A lawyer friend tells me that the use of the term 'perverse' by a court is the nearest that it gets to being rude to one of the parties in a case. The Home Secretary is a bad loser. Off she trots to the Court of Appeal. After a long deliberation by the Court of Appeal, including days when the hearing was in camera and special advocates had to be appointed, the judgment, headed not by a 'mere' judge but by the Lord Chief Justice, was confirmation that the action of the Home Secretary was perverse. He went on to say that all that having sat in secret for two or three days did was to reinforce his view that the Home Secretary's action was perverse.

I want to be generous to the Home Secretary. The Home Secretary's view was framed by – guess – this country's security and intelligence services, which peddle a line, quite confident and arrogant, that nobody is ever going to question their judgment. However, on this occasion they did, and not just Members of Parliament – including Lord Waddington, Baroness Boothroyd, Lord Russell-Johnston, a former Conservative Lord Advocate and many Members of this House – but a court of the level of the High Court and the Lord Chief Justice of England. That is a slight victory, but when there is the damning judgment that the attitude being pursued by Her Majesty's Government was 'perverse', that shows the need, in my view, for people to be able to explain their position more fully before the high court of Parliament, and to be accountable for their stewardship.

… I have two serious points that I want to share with the House … In the last decade of the South African apartheid regime period, a man called Wouter Basson was the head of the South African equivalent of Porton Down. He was described by journalists writing about the truth and reconciliation commission, in respect of which he had a big hearing, as the Dr. Mengele of South Africa. It is a matter of fact, not conjecture, that he was involved in chemical and biological research … For 10 years, he was given access to the United Kingdom. It is not unreasonable for me or any other hon. Member to ask why, and on what basis.

I tabled a parliamentary question this week asking on what basis Wouter Basson was allowed to come to the United Kingdom, and to have either the ownership or tenancy of a house in Berkshire. The Government's reply was, 'We don't discuss individual cases'. Of course, I would defend that as a general principle, but it is a matter of fact that that man was involved in serious wrongdoing both in South Africa and internationally. He was an agent of the South African apartheid regime. He was involved in chemical and biological weapons. So he must have been in the United Kingdom with the full knowledge and full consent of our security and intelligence services, and I want to know why.

I also want to know whether there was any ministerial cover for that. If there was not, it is a serious matter, and probably criminality could be involved, because of United Nations sanctions, as well as the United Kingdom law that governed such relationships. If there was ministerial cover, there is even more reason why the House should know. That illustrates how the security and intelligence services will use Ministers to not disclose that which should be disclosed, and I challenge the Government to come clean to the House on the relationship of Wouter Basson and his Project Coast.

I made a Data Protection Act request to the Foreign Office in relation to myself. I asked a lot of questions about Wouter Basson and Project Coast, and to summarise, the Minister's replies were broadly, 'There's nothing in this'. Yet when I made my Data Protection Act request, it was disclosed that 'a handling strategy meeting to deal with Andrew Mackinlay's questions' had taken place and that no fewer than 13 officials attended that meeting to give me the reply that there was nothing in it. Being a diligent Member of Parliament, I inevitably asked the next question, 'Who were the officials who attended the handling strategy meeting to deal with Andrew Mackinlay's questions about Wouter Basson and Project Coast?' And they refused to answer, because the spooks were there. That is the truth, and they know that it was true that there was some illicit, probably illegal, involvement by our security and intelligence services with Wouter Basson and the apartheid regime's chemical and biological weapons research. So they do not like that sort of question.

The other thing that I want to share with the House – I have hesitated about this – is that I, as a diligent Member of Parliament, take an interest in many parts of the world, and from time to time, as other Members of Parliament do, I meet an official from the Russian embassy, to ascertain the Russian Government's views. We cannot rely on the British press and media and certainly not on the British Government's objectivity in such matters. In my discussions, I give such state secrets as 'I think that Tony Blair will retire probably in 2007' and my firm prediction that there will be no contest for the leadership of the Labour Party. That is the extent of it. If those are state secrets, I plead guilty before the House.

What I learn from meeting a diplomat from the Russian embassy approximately three times a year is what Russia's views are on a range of things – for instance, the Helsinki accords in relation to the controversy about Kosovo. I learn its views about nuclear missile defence. I suspect that many other hon. Members do that. If they do not, they should, because at least if we understand the other guy's point of view, we can make a good assessment of how we should probe the Government and what we should be arguing and so on. For example, the British want someone extradited from Moscow, but what has not been told in the House is that Moscow would like some people extradited from London to face courts in Moscow – not a wholly illegitimate claim.

… I want to share with the House – this is why I raise it as a matter for Parliament – the fact that I was approached very formally last summer by a Minister who said, 'I've been approached by you know who, who tells me that you're meeting a person from the Russian embassy'. I was and I remain highly indignant and angry, both in my regard and for Parliament. I found the approach menacing, and bearing in mind that I meet the people from the Russian embassy in this building, it means that the security and intelligence services are monitoring not only the people who come into this building, but the hon. Members whom they meet and presumably what is discussed.

I ask the House a question: is that not an affront to Parliament? Is it not serious that there should be scrutiny of hon. Members talking to people from around the world? My view is that it is important – people have fought battles over this – that any Member of Parliament should be able to talk to whomever he likes, particularly in this building. If oversight of that starts to happen, it diminishes Parliament and is very dangerous politically.

Mr. Kevan Jones: (Durham North), (Lab) I hate to accuse my hon. Friend of being a bit naïve, but does he not live in some sort of utopia and does he not think that those other people might be interested not in what he is up to, but rather in the Russian gentleman whom he meets? Does he not think that the Moscow security services follow British diplomats and other EU diplomats around different parts of the former Soviet Union?

Andrew Mackinlay: I am not naïve about the security and intelligence services around the world. I guess that they monitor officials from a variety of embassies. I object not to that – indeed, I make the assumption that it happens – but to the approach by a Minister warning me off doing such things. That was unacceptable to me, and it remains so. I see it as a breach of my rights and duties to the House and as a Member of Parliament. Of course, I have refused to buckle on this.

I want to share with the House the fact that those conversations I have with the Russians are casual. I have not exaggerated and was not being flip. I will talk about my predictions – for what they are worth – about the United Kingdom political scene over the next few months. What I get in return is Russia's views, which I do not necessarily accept, but I then understand its views about a range of issues. If we abandon that and if we feel influenced or intimidated, that is a real diminution of our roles as legislators, and I find it intolerable. I hope that other hon. Members share my view.

I am concerned about the mere fact that other people clearly had knowledge of our discussions – times and details. I occurs to me that my hon. Friend the Member for North Durham is probably part of the establishment, but I am not and I am never going to be. Basically, there is an attempt to frighten hon. Members, as I was, and they say, 'We know that you're a perfectly good patriot and we have every confidence in you, but it would be helpful if you could let us know next time you're meeting them, and you might be able to broach one or two subjects'. I think that

that is what goes on, and it has been going on in the House for years, and I am not prepared to sign up to it.

I urge hon. Members to reflect on what I have said. We must have oversight of the security and intelligence services. Ministers must be less craven to them. The Prime Minister must be bold and go down in history as saying that he will do what happens in the United States of America, Australia, Canada, the Republic of France and every other democracy, where the legislature has control and oversight of the security and intelligence services.... I believe that we are ignoring a great danger to our liberties. We should be much more jealous of the rights and privileges of the House, which people fought for and are enshrined in the Bill of Rights.

Punishing the innocent

Gareth Peirce interviewed by Moazzam Begg

Gareth Peirce is a human rights lawyer whose long list of clients includes the Birmingham Six, the Guildford Four, Guantanamo detainees, the family of Jean Charles de Menezes, and many of the men detained without trial or under a control order in the United Kingdom. She spoke to Moazzam Begg who is himself a former Guantanamo detainee and now the spokesman for the organisation Cageprisoners which first published the exchange on its website (www.cageprisoners.com), from which we reprint these excerpts. A video of the complete interview is also available there, and DVD copies can be obtained from East London Peace and Justice. Moazzam Begg's comments and questions are in italic type and Gareth Peirce's in ordinary type.

Perhaps you don't remember, Gareth, but one of the first times I met you, you said that, it was the Irish first and I can see now it's the turn of the Muslims. This was before September 11th had taken place. Did you ever envisage that we'd be in the situation that we are today that you would have to defend people who are held without charge and without trial again?

No. I'm sure none of us, whatever observations we might have made, probably in the same way that people at the beginning of the conflict in Northern Ireland would never have envisaged thirty years of sustained nightmares. I don't think we could ever have thought that things would come to how they are now.

We both visited Northern Ireland, I think it was last year, at the opening of the Free Derry Museum and I was very taken by the powerful message that was given out at that meeting, at the opening of the museum, meeting many people, including Martin McGuinness, for the first time in my life and seeing that people now were going through the peace process, had gone through a process which began in a sense with internment, and then Bloody Sunday followed as a result of that internment. Is it correct to say that what we have today is akin to internment? Is it the same? Is it different?

I think internment, as it was imposed upon the Nationalist community, was probably the wake up call to the Nationalist movement that they had to stand up and fight. And the repression of protests against internment in particular, the civil rights marches and the murders by British soldiers of civilians on Bloody Sunday, those were the ways in which the armed conflict in fact began and fuelled volunteers enlisting because there was no other way. And I think probably looking back it would not … We're all aware that, looking back, Nationalists in Northern Ireland would now say we would never have advanced to the point of shared power in Northern Ireland had there not been an armed conflict – that's the way retrospectively history would be viewed. But equally looking back it would be seen that there would never have been an armed conflict and should never have been an armed conflict if equality and sharing of power had ever been there in the first place; so it's become a circular route of history, and the lesson, I suppose, we learn is those thirty years of conflict need never have happened and that's perhaps what is now so frighteningly clear. We needn't be in the situation we are in now, we simply need not be in it and there are so many ways in which the state is viewing people and acting towards them and implementing legislation to deal with those people that's just plain wrong and it's mad, it's a completely mad construction in relation to many of the people who are at the receiving end.

Is there a parallel? Do you see something happening at that time that is happening again? Or is it different?

If one takes the straight parallel of internment it's a pretty even equation. There was just a locking up of the wrong people as a symbolic exercise to achieve a political end. To that extent, our internment in 2001 was a very similar exercise. However, were one to be a member of the Muslim community in this country now, I think there would be a different feeling than to have been a member of the Irish community in the past, and I think that there was all along a comprehension by the politicised Irish community that allies were needed, political allies were needed, no matter the extent of the armed conflict that was raging; that somewhere along the line there needed to be a progressive, political dialogue – even if it was not with the British state, with allies: the Irish government, or Irish Americans or the worldwide community. It is much harder now, I would think, to identify political allies in the world. The allies that the Muslim community deserves to have appear to come from informed non-governmental organisations, campaigning organisations who comprehend the attack that is being made on human rights, rather than organisations, countries, regimes, administrations that comprehend that there has to be a political shift. It's more a comprehension of how the law has been distorted, that appears to be the only lifeline to hang on to, more than a way of moving towards a recognition that the world cannot go on like this; we cannot go on with this level of political and religious incomprehension. We cannot. We are in a state of grave danger.

The day I returned from Guantanamo and I met you and spoke to you, you told me the next day you could not be there with me for the interviews with the police because you told me you had to rush off to the House of Lords to issue a decision in the case of the internment, the Belmarsh detainees. I still never really understood what that meant in terms of a decision being made by the most powerful legal body in the country and then in practical, tangible terms, it meant nothing, when they were re-arrested. Can you just explain that to me?

The government had gone through a number of deceits. It had told the Council of Europe that in December 2001 this country was facing a grave emergency so that the fabric of the nation was threatened, so that a dozen men had to be locked up indefinitely without trial. That was never true. The factual claim was false for all to see. The legal claim sustained itself over three and a half years until the House of Lords ruled. That was a significant victory in a number of ways. It reaffirmed that the courts in this country were capable of assessing and delivering a profoundly moral message; that we will not stoop to that kind of legislation, we simply will not, whatever the odds. But all of that legislation came in on the excuse of 9/11, which frankly had nothing to do with this country until we made it something to do with this country. But there followed thereafter another excuse, and that was the bombings in London of July 7th 2005, five months after the interned men were released.

And were these men ever said to have any link, or any association?

No, nothing, absolutely nothing whatsoever. They were young British men, very quickly within a couple of days from Leeds known to have carried out the bombings on their own; not Arabic speakers, British nationals. There has never been any suggestion that they were motivated by, inspired by, connected with the foreign national Arabic speaking Algerians, Jordanians, Palestinians, Libyans who have been interned. Nothing to do with them. However, within days the Prime Minister again took the same group of men for his symbolic response. This country is going to face up to this grave emergency. How? By changing the rules of the game. This is what he said, changing the rules of the game. How does he do it? He will lock up these men once again and, this time, deport them to their own countries who will torture them and probably kill them. For three and a half years, he had said we can't deport them because they'll be tortured and therefore we will lock them up indefinitely without trial. Now he was saying suddenly overnight that we can …

Based on the infamous memorandums of understanding.

Although with Algeria, they didn't ever achieve a memorandum of understanding, in the end they gave up, but nevertheless the deportations were ordered. The same tiny little group of men who were there to become the scapegoats for the administration to show that they were tough on terror, shoulder to shoulder with Bush, dealing with an emergency in an utterly illogical, false, unjustified way. But it didn't really matter to the mass of this country because these were outcasts, outcasts from society. They didn't belong, they were foreigners, they had no rights – that's how in general we perceive it here.

These men have become, as you've said, outcasts and it would have been understandable had they been charged with a crime or had some evidence been put forward about them being involved in some sort of activity against the British government or in general. But that's never happened. And I remember you told me that they've not even been interrogated.

No, no they've not ever been questioned. There's much debate as to whether the police need powers to question people for 7, 14, 28, 90 days. They've never been questioned at all, never.

And the Security Services have never asked a question about them?

No, no, no, no. No, they've made an assessment. What the assessment is we don't know because the processes that have been constructed are to have courts that hear secret evidence so that the person himself will not know the evidence.

I remember when you wrote to me in Guantanamo Bay, one of the things you told me about, the Combatant Status Review Tribunal, which was this sort of kangaroo court, which didn't have any legal jurisdiction and you told me I shouldn't take part in it because it's something that includes secret evidence, you don't get witnesses, there's no appeals process – in fact there's no process, it's simply a military panel making a decision on your life. This seems to me ...

It was somewhat hypocritical of me to write that, wasn't it? Given what was happening here.

Because the lawyer also does not get the right of hearing the evidence, also.

Yes.

And this is where they determine a person's – not guilt, because they have not been charged with a crime – but a person's security threat level almost. And as a result of these secret proceedings they are either continually kept in prison or put out under a strict regime of control orders, or have placed upon them UN sanctions, or in some cases get deported or extradited. The average person would be extremely surprised to hear this, to learn that these great terrorist threats to this country have not even been questioned. How does the government respond when you ask them to produce the evidence, to say what is it that my clients have done for which they are paying this ultimate price?

Well, one discovers there's been a range of dishonesty here to get the legislation through Parliament, internment in the first place in 2001. A number of Parliamentarians quite rightly said that we have jury trial in this country, we have proper process of accusation; and they were reassured that this would also be a last resort if this legislation comes in and there will always have been a careful decision by the Crown Prosecution Service before we resort to the last resort of secret evidence. But after these men were arrested, we wrote to the Crown Prosecution Service, the Director of Public Prosecutions, and said please just tell us the dates when you took these decisions not to prosecute and who took the decision, what did they have in front of them. When the letter came back, saying actually we never took a decision at all, about any of them. So the legislation was passed on a fraudulent basis in the first place but it is sustained itself even when that legislation was condemned by the House of Lords; its message continues and its decision continues in that the same men were made the subject of control orders, released to forms of home house arrest, again on secret evidence and then some of them made available for deportation, again on secret evidence. But in fact, worse was to come, because we now have discovered that the government has sent the findings of this secret court to each regime, each torturing regime to which it wishes to send this particular group of men. It is a complete breach of every guarantee given to every asylum seeker that your application for asylum will be treated in confidence. We've sent the asylum claims to Algeria, and Jordan and probably Libya, and therefore we have placed the same hapless group of men at even further risk – we've sent their asylum claims, and we've sent the findings of SIAC – the Immigration Appeals Commission that has considered secret evidence. And when one man, Benaissa Taleb, an Algerian, went back in despair – although he was on bail here the conditions were so horrific he decided he would risk torture to leave his wife and daughter here with the ability to have a better life, in the hopes he would not be detained. He was detained; he was tortured, interrogated, charged on the basis of a false confession obtained from torture. And at his trial, the Algerian judge said, 'How dare you claim asylum in another country, that's a betrayal of our country, Algeria. It is an absolute treacherous betrayal to have claimed asylum'. So the very fact of claiming asylum …

…is itself guiltworthy. It's devastated people's lives. It's destroyed, not just the men and their ability to be men for their families, but also the effects – whether it's imprisonment without trial, whether it's the control order regime – I've spoken to several people, either the prisoners or under control orders who speak of finding this a paradox in Britain, of a country that is supposed to be one of the bastions of freedom, liberty and justice, where in fact many of them had sought asylum for that reason in the United Kingdom, and laws are being created specifically for these men; men who still have not been charged with a crime. Some of them, as you said, have opted to return home facing torture; one I've spoken to recently, Abu Rideh, is on hunger strike, has tried to harm himself, as a result of these strict measures that he has on him. His family life is completely upside down as a result of it. Is there any hope for them at all?

For a long time, probably misleadingly, not intentionally, lawyers have said to the men there is hope, this legislation can't be right. We can win internment. Control orders can't be right; we can win this in courts. Deportation to countries that torture, with memorandums of understanding, can't be right; we could win this. But the people we represent become very tired and very cynical and very disbelieving. They will say perhaps you were right but it took three and a half years for internment to be overturned. Perhaps you were right about deportation, but we have been in prison now for three years – another three years, on top of the three and a half from internment. And those men will say even if we win, look at the cost to our families or to the community and – even more cynically – if we win, the government will simply introduce something else. So the prospect of normality of life has become nil and it's an endurance test in which the government has all the time in the world on its side and men see their lives disappearing; young men who are single see no prospect of ever being able to marry and have a family; men who are married with children, see the children growing up without fathers at all; or with fathers at home in circumstances that are destructive of a normal family life. I think, to be frank, people given a choice would never, never want to be here. Refugees would never have chosen to come here if they'd ever known this was ahead of them and if there were any prospect of another country, a safe third country, no one would be here for a moment. But what we're doing is meant to be sending a message to the world, isn't it? We're not acting only in relation to our domestic borders; we're trying to encourage other countries to behave in the same way.

I had a meeting with a judge, a judge advocate, a general from the US military about three weeks ago. He was so adamant that detainees' cases in Guantanamo could be won, through fighting their case in the court and ultimately to the Supreme Court. In fact, he felt so confident that the tie he had on which had Supreme Court frontages on it, he took off during dinner and gave it to me. And I thought to myself, no one has been released from Guantanamo as the result of any legal proceeding, even when the Supreme Court decision was passed in Rasul vs Bush. But at least in the cases in Guantanamo and in my case in particular, when you were working on it, there was a public outcry, eventually. And that is what ended up securing or bringing about our release to the embarrassment and so forth, but in the case of the men here who are held, not in similar circumstances, but under similar attitudes of the law, or of the government, where they don't have the right to challenge their detention; why is it that the public simply – to be as blunt as possible – doesn't give a damn?

We're a pretty apathetic country politically. We're a pretty xenophobic country. It's always an easy populous message to wave the flag of no more immigrants, no more refugees, enough's enough. And if you add that basic concept to terrorism then the equation's complete. These are people that the nation were being encouraged to think no country would want within their borders; countries made to think these are dangerous people. As no one has ever talked to them I can't see how any one can properly assess what they are. But those who are detained, or not detained, some of whom you have met, many of whom I have met, talking to them, we're quite capable of seeing that they are people who are not a threat – far from it. If we had some ability to talk intelligently and sensibly to people who are themselves intelligent and sensible we might find that this country is simply looking in the wrong direction. And if there is to be any hope or prospect of the world becoming a safer, saner place, it has to be on a basis of comprehension and understanding. And at the present moment that is spectacularly missing. I am sure you see that far more vividly than I.

When peace eventually came to Northern Ireland, they had to negotiate with those very same members they had demonised and said were the leaders of the terrorist movements, and cells and the political wings and so forth. And bizarrely before Tony Blair left, one of his lasting actions, I suppose, will be that he was the man who brought Martin McGuiness and Ian Paisley together – and still it seems bizarre. Yet we're looking at some of the people we've just mentioned, who are not involved and never been charged with being involved in any acts of terrorism in this country – they are clearly in some cases dissidents from their countries, because that's how they and why they sought political asylum here. But the government makes it look as if these people are not only part of the problem, but they are the problem. But based on the Northern Ireland example, are they not really part of the solution?

I would have thought that any sane intelligent person could comprehend that, but I think it's not just talking to the people themselves and finding out that they are not as painted, that's one thing. But the second aspect that's missing is that what those people are representative of; as you say, they are dissidents, opposed to the regimes from which they've fled – no doubt about it, and justifiably so. We're talking about regimes that torture people, that kill people, that commit genocide, where hundreds of thousands of people are disappeared, countries that are recipients and agents of the American rendition programme. Those are the regimes we're talking about. And one of the men who is relied upon significantly as a focus of the legislation, what did he do to attract the condemnation of his country, Jordan? He protested against the invasion of Kuwait by Saddam

Hussein. He was the voice in Jordan that said Jordan should not have supported Saddam Hussein, as it did. And for that he was tortured and for that he was perceived as a dissident and fled. Now it seems to me that there is a wilful and deliberate unethical foreign policy here, in that for our own economic and strategic reasons, we embrace these torturing regimes, and therefore we are in the position where those regimes complain, as they have vociferously, that their dissidents are here; we then move against them in the name of the War on Terror. But to achieve a world order that is just, we cannot forever uphold those regimes, we cannot forever support them. We fail to understand that the world conflicts that are the most insoluble must be solved and they become solved by some form of comprehension. We are just slavishly following a path of incomprehension, and these men who are here are simply part and parcel of that incomprehension.

A great number of the men who have been detained under these anti-terror legislation measures or been put under these control orders are actually from Libya. And I think that's an important case in point, because it demonstrates how many of these Libyan men were given asylum readily by the United Kingdom over the past couple of decades; and then all of a sudden, after the War on Terror an agreement is made between Gaddafi's Libya, who was a pariah for the last thirty to forty years, and now all of a sudden has become relatively friendly between the United Kingdom and the United States of America. It's nothing to do with justice. It's all to do with interests. How does one explain that, as somebody who lives under a control order regime, for example, when everybody he knows, everybody he deals with on a day to day basis he has to inform that I'm under this control order regime and therefore the warning lights come on? How can he explain that interests have changed, I have remained the same, I've never changed at all? Can he do that at all?

There is an element in going through the motions of legal representation before SIAC, before the administrative court of control orders, where all of it seems so nonsensical. You're talking about whether there should be a boundary drawn around a premises in Leicester that allows a Libyan dissident to go to one gym or another gym. It's all completely barking mad. We're talking about young men, or once young men, who, in anybody's view, courageously stood up to this outrageous tyrant, who is also insane – Gaddafi – who stood up, who protested, who said this regime should not continue. And now their lives are to be conducted with geographical lines drawn around. They are not a threat to national security. It is mad to assess them with this. And yet we're so far down the road of the rubber stamp from internment being applied to control orders, being applied to deportation, that there's no longer any capacity for anyone to stand up and say the Emperor has no clothes on – at all.

Yes, that's true. One of the other things that came out, after the September 11th attacks, in the legislation in the United Kingdom, is this fast track or supposed fast track extradition treaty with the United States of America which is non reciprocal. It has caused great consternation amongst the Muslim community in the case of Babar Ahmad and others. Is there any merit in this at all? Is there any merit, as far as the Americans are concerned? Is there a real case that somebody can somehow after all of these years, will a person like Babar Ahmad, or Haroon, or any of the other guys that are under extradition, will they ever be able to rightfully defend themselves if that ever transpires, if they are ever extradited?

They are not meant to be able to properly defend themselves. What they will face when they go there is being detained in isolation, under special measures, imposed on them pre-trial, which will pretty much break any strong human being. If they're convicted, they will probably spend the rest of their natural lives in identical situations, virtual isolation in a Supermax prison. The evidence against them will be constructed from corrosive methodology in which witnesses for the prosecution are encouraged to become witnesses by threats; if you don't do this, you will be made an enemy combatant and locked up in Guantanamo, or in a military brig; or yourself get life imprisonment without parole. The prospects are horrific and the men here fighting extradition know it. The only advantage, slight advantage, is that this greedy American extension of its jurisdiction has come to embrace the banking community here and therefore bankers are getting sent. British Aerospace employees are being questioned now because we in this country stopped a prosecution for corrupt payments to Saudi Arabia by British Aerospace. That is now becoming an area of interest for American prosecution. There is going to be an awful lot of squealing going on if our upper echelons of business are vulnerable to American prosecution. But the argument is the same: if there is a proper prosecution to be brought the natural forum should be the country in which the person lives and from which the evidence is gained. In the case of Babar Ahmad, that will be here. The man was allegedly running a website, with a collective of people of Islamic interests, and simply because the service provider was arbitrarily based in Connecticut his extradition is now sought for trial in Connecticut.

That's his only link to the United States.

He's never been to Connecticut. The whole of the readership of Azzam.com, which was the website, was cyberspace, worldwide, anyone could have a look. But it's Connecticut that's after him. But it's this appetite, this same appetite that kidnapped you and took you to Guantanamo; America *über alles*, America the Superpower, America has the right and the ability to make everyone subject to it.

Yes, often I say I've never been to America – America came to me.

It did.

Through extraordinary rendition. Babar has never been to Connecticut but he may be sent there through extradition, which almost sounds like extraordinary rendition. What is the prospect for all of these people, all these people detained under these measures? The common denominator of course is that they are detained without charge or trial. And even people who have been charged or convicted of crimes, today we can see for example someone can be convicted of writing poetry, convicted of downloading something from the internet – that's a significant change from the time of the Troubles in Northern Ireland. Is there any precedent for that sort of thing that you've ever seen before? Thought crimes?

There were aspects of that in a way. Look, the IRA was a military organisation carrying out military campaigns, setting off bombs, murders, kidnaps. You could know what was being done. You could arrest, you could prosecute for substantive offences. There was a subtext as well that attempted to be censorship which was a pretty spectacular failure, with broadcasting ban, ludicrous. But it was seen as ludicrous and in a way the Nationalist community gained some strength from that. This is more worrying because it's so confusing, it's so inscrutable, it's going backwards. I know when you came back from Guantanamo, and we were talking about the fact people were being interned and what for. Well, insofar as they knew it was because they supported Chechen resistance. And you commented, 'Oh, has that become a crime since I've been gone?' Well, the answer is it never was a crime, it isn't a crime but it is somehow being devolved into being a crime, in the sense it's terrorism now. Self-defence or self-determination has been twisted into being terrorism, by somehow attaching liberation struggles through expanding definitions into something that is criminalised. And that is utter confusion. If one was a lawyer and someone came to you and said, is it a crime for me to support a resistance struggle. You would say, no, the United Nations Declaration of Independence tells you that you can. The United Nations Declaration of Human Rights tells you that it's appropriate to overthrow a tyrant as a last resort, it's appropriate to support an entity that is able to claim self-determination. That's all gone by the board – the definition of terrorism now says all of that is a crime. Any attempt to overthrow any government anywhere in the world is now terrorism, and therefore it's all a political decision on the part of our government as to what it will go after and what it won't. And who can know where they stand? People go to lawyers and say if I publish this book, if I put up this website, is it legal or not? He will say in theory it's legal, but in practice it well could be a crime, and so there is no certainty. And people, there are many people in prison now who haven't a clue why they are there, absolutely no idea; and there are some young people convicted who do not know, do not understand why they've been convicted. They've searched the internet, they've looked at things, they've left a trace on their computer and suddenly that's a crime …

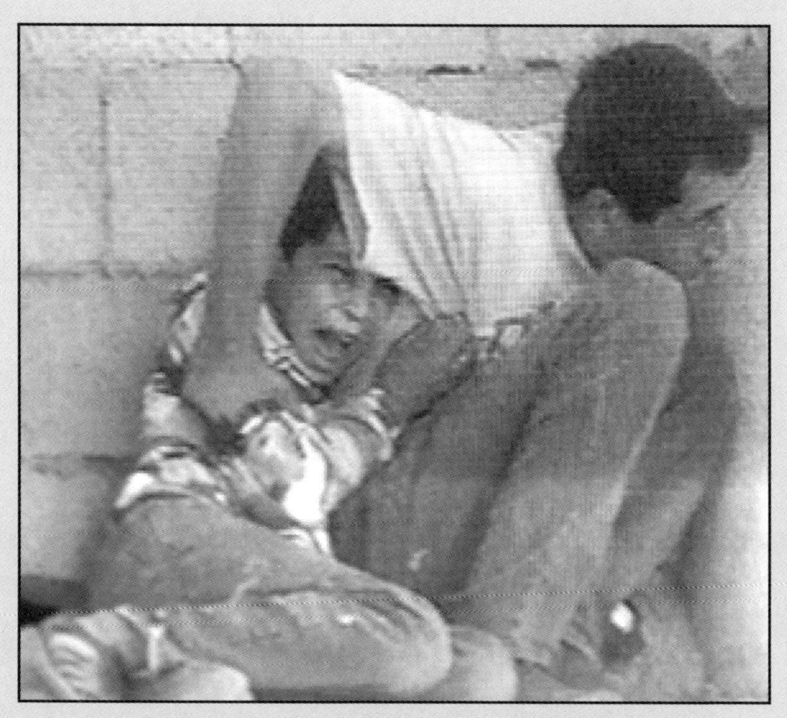

Mohammad

Mahmoud Darwish

Darwish's Requiem for Mohammad Al-Dura, the 12-year-old boy shot by Israeli soldiers as he was stranded with his father at Netzarim Junction in Gaza, was published in September 2000. The shooting was caught on camera and broadcast widely in the days after it happened.

Nestled in his father's arms, a bird
afraid of the hell above him, Mohammad prays:
Father, protect me from flying.
My wing is weak against the wind,
and the light is black.

Mohammad wants to go home,
without a bicycle, without a new shirt.
He wants his school desk and his book
of grammar. Take me home, father, so I can finish
my homework and complete my years slowly,
slowly on the seashore and under the palms.
Nothing further.
Nothing beyond.

Mohammad faces an army, without a stone, without
the shrapnel of stars. He did not see the wall
where he could write: 'My freedom will
not die.' He has, as yet, no freedom,
no horizon for a single Picasso dove.
He is still being born. He is still
being born into the curse of his name.
How often should a boy be born without a childhood or a country?
And where will he dream, when the dream comes to him,
and the earth is a wound and an altar?

Mohammad sees his death approach
and remembers a moment from TV
when a tiger stalking a nursing fawn
shied away upon smelling the milk,
as if milk tames a beast of prey.
And so I am going to be saved, says the boy,
and he weeps. My life is there, hidden

in my mother's closet. I will be saved . . .
I can see it.

Mohammad,
hunters are gunning down angels, and the only witness
is a camera's eye
watching a boy become one
with his shadow.
His face like the sunrise, clear.
His heart like an apple, clear.
His ten fingers like candles, clear.
And the dew on his trousers, clear.
His hunter could have thought:
I'll leave him
until he can spell 'Palestine',
I'll pawn him tomorrow,
kill him when he rebels.

Mohammad,
small Christ, where you sleep and dream
is itself an icon
made of olive branches and brass
and a people who are rising up.
Mohammad,
blood superfluous to prophets and prophecies,
so to the right side of heaven ascend,
O Mohammad.

Translated by Tania Tamari Nasir

Nothing for the Hungry

Jean Ziegler
An interview

Jean Ziegler was the UN Special Rapporteur on the Right to Food from 2000 to 2008. He is now a Member of the UN Human Rights Council's Advisory Committee. He is the author of Empire of Shame: The Fight against Poverty and Oppression.

In June 2008, Professor Ziegler gave a radio interview about the outcome of the Conference on World Food Security: The Challenges of Climate Change and Bioenergy, which had just met at the UN Food and Agricultural Organisation's Headquarters in Rome. The questions are in italics and Professor Ziegler's replies in ordinary type.

On the last day of the World Food Conference, the non-governmental organisation World Hunger Help made a sharp criticism: the Conference had not resulted in a binding common agreement on the development of agriculture and the rural regions in the world. Only short-term measures for reducing the prices of fertilizers and seeds were decided, a change which will result in even greater dependency on the part of small farmers ... Mr. Ziegler, at first sight it seems a good idea that the United Nations sets its sights on cheaper seeds and cheaper fertilizers, doesn't it? What's wrong with that?

This summit, in which 50 heads of government participated as well as more than 2,000 diplomats, ended in a really scandalous way. I think that World Hunger Help is absolutely right, and almost all NGOs are of the same opinion: this is a victory for the corporations, who dominate over 80 per cent of the world's agricultural trade. Day by day 100,000 people are dying from hunger or its immediate consequences; every five seconds a child under the age of ten is starved. And instead of fighting hunger, which is claiming more and more victims, food price explosion even increases the hunger, this very massacre, as one of the NGOs put it clearly in Rome.

The Rome summit tends to even increase the hunger in the world instead of really fighting it. Why is this so? The conclusions, the recommendations and final resolution of the Rome summit result in nothing else but more market liberalisation. That means there will be even more dumping of agricultural goods. The big companies can sell their products to the agrarian countries of the southern hemisphere even more easily, and these countries will have no chance to react against this by means of customs barriers or contingents, and so on.

So, if fertilizers, seeds, etc will become cheaper, this does not mean that basic foodstuffs will also become cheaper in the poor countries?

Definitely not! The primary goal would be to protect their agriculture. Last year the industrial nations, members of the Organisation for Economic Co-operation and Development and the 27 European Union countries paid common production and export subsidies amounting to 345 billion dollars. On every African market you can buy European vegetables and fruit for half the price or even one-third the price of the domestic products of equal quality. And this price dumping is what is destroying their domestic agriculture.

Many had expected that at least there would be resolutions concerning biofuels, concerning the use of land for the production of biofuels instead of food products, on which people can be fed. But there was no resolution of that kind. What are the reasons?

The reason is the absolute weakness of the present United Nations Secretary General who – and I am expressing myself very cautiously – is very much exposed to US influence. Therefore he did not recommend anything that could bother the corporations in the least. You are definitely right in saying that it is a crime to burn hundreds of millions of tons of corn – last year it amounted to 138 million tons of corn which in the United States alone were used to produce bioethanol or diesel, while human beings in the world are going hungry. This is a crime and should be prohibited altogether. Such a prohibition wasn't even dealt with in Rome, only a vague recommendation was expressed to the effect that research in this field should be promoted so that one day other means of production might be available. So this was an absolute step backwards and it was a betrayal of the United Nations Charter which lays down solidarity and help for the poorest and respect for the principle of 'food for all' on this planet.

Source: www.currentconcerns.ch

Roots of Hunger

James Petras

James Petras is a Bartle Professor (Emeritus) of Sociology at Binghamton University, New York. His new book is called Zionism, Militarism and the Decline of US Power *(Clarity Press).*

In recent times, all the major international banks (IMF, World Bank, Inter-American Development Bank, Asia Development Bank, and so on), all the major financial newspapers and mass media have been forced to recognize that there is a major food crisis, that hundreds of millions of people face hunger, malnutrition and outright starvation.

> *'The world's poor countries will spend about $38.7 billion dollars importing cereals this year, double the amount they paid two years ago for the same amounts and a 57% increase from 2007.'*
>
> *Quote from US Senator Byron Dorgan at the United Nations Food and Agricultural Organization (UN FAO), Financial Times, 21 April 2008*

World conferences have been convoked, national emergencies have been declared as millions riot in nearly 50 countries, and threaten to overthrow regimes and mass social tensions rise even in the most dynamic, high-growth countries like China and India. Even in the imperialist countries in North America and Europe, skyrocketing food prices, combined with stagnant wages, home evictions and debt payments threaten incumbent regimes and increase pressures on all governments to take urgent action.

The élite responses are predictably inadequate, and their explanations for the crisis range from inadequate, self-serving, to silly. The World Bank repeats the call for emergency food aid, and several hundred million dollar grants to the 'most needy' – those countries where there have been major food riots, sacking private food distributors, private wholesale and retail outlets, and threatening or ousting free market regimes who have been the model pupils of the World Bank and International Monetary Fund policies.

The self-styled economic experts predictably make asses of themselves trying to evade the failure of their past prescriptions. Conservatives and liberal and progressive academics and policy advisers all blame 'China for eating too much meat' (Professor Paul Krugman of Princeton University and *New York Times* columnist), the 'growth of demand', 'inflation'; the progressives point to the diversion of production to bio-fuels 'ethanol' and 'bio-diesel', or to 'the lack of government planning and the distortion of priorities'.

The increased food aid has yet to have anything but momentary impact, in limited regions, on a fraction of the affected population. Pointing the finger at the growth of demand begs the question of the 'lack of supply', and the structural features (land tenure, profit seeking, ownership patterns and state-class relations), which shape it. Equally important, even where foodstuffs arrive at the market, they are priced out of reach for the majority of urban and rural workers, peasants and the unemployed. The supply-demand critics fail to apply a class analysis of the 'producers' who determine the price system (according to their oligopolistic market power and criteria for profits) and the consumers (informal and poorly paid formal workers with declining income). Capitalist farmers are in a position to protect and even increase their profits by passing added costs for inputs on to the weaker market power of the consumers, aided and abetted by the neo-liberal free market political regimes.

The progressives who blame bio-fuels for the food crisis (higher prices resulting from the diversion of grains and land use to fuel production) fail to address the most elementary structural questions: what classes came to state power and fashioned the economic policies which enabled the 'diversion' to take place? Heavy private and state borrowing in the 1970s due to the availability of cheap credit led to the growth of indebtedness. Indebted private banks, businesses and manufacturers, real estate developers, through powerful influence and direct links to the state, foisted their private debts onto the state and ultimately onto the taxpayers, what was later described as 'socializing the private debt' or 'bailing out the private sector'.

The state, faced with mounting debt obligations – the so-called 'debt crisis' –, turned to the IMF and World Bank to secure loans and, more important, to gain their certification for jumbo loans from commercial banks. The IMF and World Bank demanded fundamental structural changes from the state to grant loans. These conditional loans involved a comprehensive transformation in investment, trade, consumption and income policies, which had a major impact on the class structure and the composition of the ruling class.

The international loans, both official and commercial, and the structural changes which accompanied them, led to the elimination of protective trade barriers in agriculture and manufacturing. As a result, there was a massive inflow of subsidized agricultural commodities from the US and the European Union, which destroyed small and medium size family farm producers of basic foodstuffs. The bankruptcy of food producers led to massive displacements of farmers and farm workers to the cities and the concentration of land in the hands of agro-business plantation owners who concentrated on growing crops for export.

The IMF and World Bank demands included the re-allocation of state credit, loans and technical assistance toward big agro-exporters in single commodities because they earned hard currency needed to pay back loans and for profit remittances of the multinational corporations back to their stock holders, directors and owners.

The IMF and World Bank agreed to negotiate the roll over of impending interest and principal payments of debtor states on condition that they privatize and de-nationalize all lucrative and monopoly state enterprises. Privatizations and de-nationalization led to large-scale foreign takeovers of vast tracts of rich agricultural lands and grain production and exports by local landed oligarchs and foreign investors.

These policies eliminating trade barriers, and promoting privatization and de-nationalizations, the deep penetration of markets and production sectors, and the heightened emphasis of state intervention on behalf of export-oriented foreign exchange earnings economic activity was dubbed 'neo-liberalism'. This model was a combination of state directed and regulated socio-economic policies designed to enhance the role and power of foreign and domestic élites oriented toward specialized world markets.

The ascendancy of this new power configuration during the 1980s and 1990s dictated the key political and economic decisions regarding investments (their allocations, their sector and sub-sector) as well as the markets (internal and external) and the products (foods, fuels, staples) and pricing (oligopolistic cartels). The basic principle guiding the new foreign and domestic ruling classes was to specialize in complementary activity within the world economy (what orthodox economists call 'specialization based on comparative advantages'). The integration of foreign and local ruling classes was mutually supportive and lucrative: private capital and commodities traversed their international commodity and financial circuits.

The large-scale, middle term consequences of this new power configuration for agriculture, food production and prices manifested itself in a little over a decade. By the second half of the first decade of the 21st century an unprecedented agricultural crisis erupted: the ascendancy of the agro-export sector of the ruling class and the implementation of their 'free market' agenda led to the end of price controls and the skyrocketing of prices. Prices reflected the social relations of production and distribution: big capitalist farmer dominance of land and investment shaped 'supply' and wholesale prices; giant global commercial retailers ('supermarkets') set direct consumer prices. There was 'competition' between oligopolist producers and distributors over who could secure the highest prices and biggest profits.

The ruling class agro-exporters ended subsidies for family farmer food producers and increased export subsidies for staple producers. Family farmers were bankrupted and their land was bought up by real estate speculators (self-styled 'developers') for commercial uses, golf courses, resorts, luxury gated communities and export staples. Rice fields were turned into country clubs. Wheat and corn prices doubled in the course of the ten months between September 2007 and July 2008. Profits 'fatten(ed) Cargill's balance sheet' (*Financial Times,* 15 April 2008): quarterly profits went up 86% to $1.03 billion dollars in the third quarter ending 29 February 2008. It was not simply, as the orthodox pundits would have it, that 'demand' was up, but that hundreds of billions of speculator monies poured into commodity markets. Under conditions of tightly controlled markets by big agribusiness, grain stocks fell to their lowest levels in 35 years relative to demand, largely because big agro-capital sought to limit supply of food and increase production of fuel, and diverted capital to commodity speculation. As a result of the ascendancy of giant agro-capitalist rule, and their investment and land use policies, average food prices rose by 45% between July 2007 and April 2008, and are projected to rise by an additional 15% by July.

Frightened more by mass protests toppling compliant client regimes than mass hunger and rising mortality of the poor, the capitalist leaders from around the world met in Washington in the spring of 2008. They whined about the food riots and moaned over the 'loss of a decade's progress (sic) in Africa' and even called for 'action'. As could be expected, a few hundred million in emergency food aid was promised, destroying the last bastions of small-scale farmers producing food for the local market. Neo-liberal regimes throughout Asia were frightened into blocking exports of basic food items in order to prevent food riots turning into mass insurrections: wages and salaries lagged behind accelerating food prices. The neo-liberal regimes of Indonesia, Egypt, India, Vietnam, China and Cambodia banned foreign sales of rice (*Financial Times,* 16 April 2008). Yet these protectionist gestures and food handouts have had little positive effect at home and have exacerbated scarcities for food importers. Corn futures hit a record $6.16 dollars a bushel between January and March 2008, a 30% increase. Indonesia's export ban raised the price of rice 63% during the first three months of 2008.

None of the world leaders meeting in Washington 'concerned' about hunger, regression and, most of all, revolutions, proposed agrarian reform – redistributing land to peasants and farmers to produce food. None of the leaders even proposed reforms such as price and profit controls and the re-conversion of land use to agricultural production. None of these leaders proposed outlawing speculation in commodity futures in the world bourses. It is no wonder that the IMF 'predicts' food prices will continue rising until 2010.

The fuel prices have not been reduced with the triple digit increase in ethanol production. Ethanol (and fuel) and food prices have increased despite expansion of production because the same monopoly power configuration operates in both sectors.

The wage-price gap is structural immiseration. The mass protests, in the Third as well as the imperial countries, are over immediate basic problems. But their roots are embedded in the deep structures of the capitalist economy.

Only mindless prestigious orthodox economists employed by the Central Banks still prattle about 'core' and 'headline inflation' – as if food, fuel, health and education price increases are not central to everyday life for billions of lives. Even worse they fail to understand that rampant inflation and stagnant incomes are deeply embedded in the very structures of capitalist economy and state. What is absolutely clear is the bankruptcy of the theory of export product specialization at the expense of food security. What was a demand of a radical minority is now at the top of the agenda for a multi-billion person movement.

People are demanding a u-turn from the disastrous Friedmanite theories of relying on monopolized world food markets to a return of revolutionary policies of food self-sufficiency.

From Judgment to Calculation

Mike Cooley

Mike Cooley, engineer, academic and activist is well known to Spokesman *readers for his pivotal role in the internationally acclaimed Lucas Workers' Corporate Plan. His work has been translated into more than twenty languages, and his awards and distinctions include joint winner of the $50,000 Alternative Nobel Prize, which he donated to socially useful design projects.*

This article first appeared in AI and Society *Vol 21 No. 4 June 2007: an international journal of human-centred systems which Mike helped to establish in 1987.*

Information technology (IT) systems frequently come between the professional and the primary task as the real world of touch, shape, size, form (and smell) is replaced by an image on a screen or a stream of data or calculation outputs. This can lead to high levels of abstraction where the ability to judge is diminished. I have described elsewhere the case of a designer using an advanced computer aided design (CAD) system who input the decimal point one place to the right and downloaded the resultant output to the production department on a computer-to-computer basis (Cooley 1991). The seriousness of this error was further exacerbated when the designer, shown the resulting component which had been produced, did not even recognise that its dimensions were ten times too large.

Scientific knowledge and mathematical analysis enter into engineering in an indispensable way and their role will continue. However, engineering contains elements of experience and judgment, regard for social considerations and the most effective way of using human labour. These partly embody knowledge which has not been reduced to exact and mathematical form. 'They also embody value judgments which are not amenable to the scientific method.' (Rosenbrock 1977).

These will be significant issues as IT is increasingly deployed in societal areas such as that of healthcare. Cases already abound and many have become high profile public issues, e.g. the paediatricians who administered a fatal dose of 15 mg of morphine instead of the correct 0.15 mg for the baby (Rogers 1999; Joseph 1999). They did this in spite of being warned by a staff nurse that the dose was obviously incorrect.

Those introducing the avalanche of new technologies frequently limit their considerations to first order outcomes. These usually declare the positive and beneficial features, whilst only fleeting attention is given to the downside, if at all. It is as if the laws of thermodynamics no longer apply and that you can get something for nothing. We are now beginning to learn, to our cost, that there are 'no free dinners' with technology. For too long we have ignored the double edged nature of science and technology. Viewed in this light, it has produced the beauty of the Taj Mahal and the hideousness of Chernobyl, the caring therapy of Röntgen's X-rays and the destruction of Hiroshima, the musical delights of Mozart and the stench of Bergen Belsen.

Most technologies display positive and negative aspects. There is now an urgent need for a new category of competence – an ability to discern the positive and negative aspects of a given technology and to build upon the positive whilst mitigating the negative features. It is not a question of being for or against technology, but rather discerning the positive and beneficial uses of it.

One negative aspect of IT technology is the under-valorisation and frequently the squandering of our society's most precious asset which is the creativity, skill and commitment of its people. Over the past 21 years *AI and Society* has facilitated a debate on positive alternatives to the existing developments and has placed particular emphasis on the potential for human centred systems. Its articles, reports and the conferences it has facilitated have provided practical examples and case studies of systems design which celebrate human talents.

It requires courage, tenacity and profound insights to develop these alternatives in our obsessively technocratic and machine centred culture.

The wow factor

Technology in its multi-various forms is rapidly becoming all pervasive. It permeates just about every aspect of what we do and who we are. It ranges from the gigantic, such as the diversion of rivers and the repositioning of mountains to the microscopic level of genetic engineering. Science fiction becomes reality as faces are transplanted and head transplants are confidently predicted.

The 'wow!' factor is mind-blowing. Even simple internet procedures have a God-like quality. With Google Globe you can look down on our planet and travel over continents and countries, quickly homing in on an aerial view of your beloved 'homestead' showing your own car in the drive.

We now appear as masters of the universe, able to see everything and confident in the belief that any problem we create we can also solve. It is just a question of a plentiful flow of research grants and resources. Meantime, we plan to bury our nuclear waste.

Awesome capability

We are the only species ever to have it within its power to destroy itself along with our beautiful and frail planet. This is an awesome capability and one for which our culture, education and politics ill prepare us to cope creatively. Change is frequently and thoughtlessly portrayed as progress, and progress so unidimensionally defined is evident on all sides.

In spite of this, at no time in history have so many people been fearful of the developments surrounding them and are becoming alienated from the society producing them. Doubts are jolted into concerns by global warming events or the looming spectre of an Avian Flu pandemic. Yet it tends to be a fear that dare not speak its name. Who after all, can be against progress, even if it is defined in its own self serving terms?

Paths not taken

In order to analyse where we are now with IT systems it is important to look back historically to identify turning points at which technology might have and could have developed differently. This is akin to Rosenbrock's notion of the 'Lushai Hills Effect' (Rosenbrock 1988, 1990). He suggests that with technology, we sometimes take a particular route of development and once we have done so we begin to believe that it is the only one. We then develop cultural forms, educational systems and a philosophical outlook which supports that contention. It therefore seems useful at this juncture to explore different interpretations of human and technological progress which may throw light on our present dilemma and indicate alternatives worthy of exploration.

Ego smashing events

We are indebted to Mazlish (1967) for the notion of technological and scientific development as dismantling discontinuities in historical ego smashing events. The first arises from Copernicus and Galileo which resulted in a re-organisation of the universe with our earth no longer at its centre. The second is based on Darwin who robbed human beings of the particular privilege of having been specially created. The third, based on

Freudian insights, suggests that we are not the masters of our own consciousness in the way we had assumed ourselves to be. Our society is now apparently demolishing the fourth discontinuity – the one between humans and their machines.

Self elimination

'To put it bluntly, we are now coming to realise that man and the machines he has created are continuous and that the same conceptual systems that help to explain the workings of the human brain also explain the workings of a thinking machine. Man's pride and his refusal to acknowledge this continuity is the sub-stratum upon which the distrust of technology and industrial society has been reared' (Mazlish 1967). However, as we shall suggest later, this sub-stratum of distrust may be overcome if we view human beings and their machines as constituting a symbiosis rather than a convergence. Otherwise, as Karl Pearson (cited in Weizenbaum 1976) puts it: 'The scientific man has above all things, to strive at self elimination in his judgments' (Pearson 1976).

Walking, feeding, thinking

Another conceptual framework which yields interesting insights is to consider technological change as a series of phyla. Rapoport (1963) identifies four. The first phylum consists of tools. Tools appear functionally as extensions of our limbs. While some mechanical advantage may be gained from such a device, it in no way functions 'independently of us'.

The second phylum is mechanical 'clockworks'. Here the human effort in winding up the mechanism is stored as potential energy which may be released. Over a long period of time the clockwork gives the impression of autonomous activity. Furthermore, it is not a prosthetic device to extend our human capabilities but rather one that produces time: hours, minutes … to pico-seconds. Thus in his seminal work, Lewis Mumford asserts that it is the clock and not the steam engine that is 'the key machine of the modern age' as it 'dissociated time from human events and helped create the belief in an independent world of mathematically measurable sequences: the special world of science' (Mumford 1963).

Weizenbaum points out that clocks 'are the first autonomous machines built by man and until the advent of the computer they remained the only truly important ones'. He also asserts 'This rejection of direct experience was to become one of the principal characteristics of modern science' (Weizenbaum 1976).

The third phylum is heat engines. These gradually emerged as devices that were neither pushed nor pulled but 'fed'. The fourth phylum covers devices capable of collecting, storing, transmitting, manipulating, initiating information and determining actions based on these.

It will be seen that in each phylum, the device moves toward autonomous capabilities but there is also a form of narcissism – technological narcissism – as clockworks 'walk', heat engines 'feed' and computers 'think'. We design devices with some human attributes and then in a strange dialectical way we begin to perceive ourselves as partial mirror images of the machines. During the early stages of clockworks, drawings showed human sinews and muscles in machine-like manner and Déscartes refers to the human being as a machine. In the era of heat engines there is a growing concern about what and how humans are fed. This is sometimes reflected in concerns about dietary intake and some even suggest could lead to anorexia.

The fourth phylum leads to a situation where someone could say disparagingly 'The human mind is the only computer made by amateurs' and a high priest of technology was presumably half joking when he said 'Human beings will have to accept their true place in the evolutionary hierarchy: animals, human beings and intelligent machines'.

Fault in reality

The foregoing provides an interesting context in which to view the potential for human centred systems. However, the discussion of such systems has suffered from its questioning of the given orthodoxy in contemporary science. To do so is to elicit the disapproval of many of one's colleagues. Sympathetic colleagues may imply that you have not grasped the greatness of all that is going on. Less sympathetic colleagues hint that you are questioning rationality itself and are therefore guilty of irrationality.

Although Stalinistic psychiatric wards are not threatened, grants may dry up and you can forget that tenured post. Perhaps the students in the sixties had a point with their posters: 'Don't adjust your mind. There's a fault in reality'.

Our culture conveys the sense that a calculation is precise, analytical and scientific. It is regarded as apolitical and objective. Indeed in the sixties, when social scientists were struggling to gain acceptance of their science, many of their papers were awash with calculations and diagrams. However, when I worked in the aerospace industry I found that those who could make best use of computers and calculations already knew in a 'ball park' sense what the answer should be and they used computer based calculation as a fine tuning device. They were able to rely on their judgment, so if a discrepancy arose the problem would be re-visited.

In spite of this, judgment tends to be regarded as something much less significant. An informed guess – or worse a shot in the dark – is often dismissed as mere speculation. At the level of proficiency, Dreyfus refers to it as 'holistic similarity recognition' and points out that 'intuition is the product of deep situational involvement and recognition of similarity'. This becomes expertise when 'not only situations but also associated decisions are intuitively understood' (Dreyfus and Dreyfus 1986). Using still more intuitive skills the expert can cope with uncertainties and unforeseen or critical situations and has the ability to override or disagree with calculated solutions.

Decision making is probably at its best when there is a creative interaction between judgment and calculation. Both have their place in the symbiosis.

Intimidation

Pivotal to all of this must be whether the output of a calculation is correct and how we can verify its status. Calculations, at least in the temporary sense, can be quite intimidating even if they are completely wrong. Archbishop Ussher, in calculating the age of the world as understood in the Middle Ages, declared it was created in 4004 BC on October 22 at about 6.00p.m. (Ussher cited in Rosenbrock 2002). Although his calculation was wrong by some billions of years it must have seemed quite impressive at the time.

Recently, in a widely publicised trial, the expert witness Sir Roy Meadows declared the probability of two natural unexplained cot deaths occurring in a family was 73 million to 1. The court was impressed. Only later, when the odds were shown to be closer to two hundred to one, was the enormity of the error exposed.

I have described elsewhere the shift from judgment to calculation with some of the consequences. Initially, these were in the engineering field but are increasingly occurring elsewhere, e.g. in the medical field. I have represented this graphically as a shift from judgment to calculation; from the subjective to the objective and from signal to noise (Cooley 2002).

The question may arise as to whether this matters significantly. Perhaps the problems identified are merely transitional ones which occur as the systems are being bedded down. It will be argued by many that this is in the nature of the human progress project.

After all, we extended the capacity of our hands through a variety of tools. With spectacles, telescopes, microscopes and scanners we extend our vision. IT technology is merely a further development in which we now extend the capacity of our minds. This is a part of human progress – a speeded up version of the strongest of the tribe climbing to the top of the hill to see what is on the other side. If it could be done then do it!

Can we, should we?

I hold that it is no longer adequate to ask 'Can we do it?' Rather we need to enquire 'Should we do it?' The fourth phyla is of a different order to the previous three.

The new technologies under consideration have been developed by appropriating human intelligence and objectivising it into computer based programmes and technological procedures. However, this is becoming qualitatively different from previous technological developments in that more and more humans – even at the highest professional levels – are becoming increasingly dependent on calculations and systems output.

The deep problem arises when human abilities and judgments so atrophy that we are incapable of disagreeing with, questioning or modifying a system's output. A simple example of this is the increasing number of people unable to add a column of figures, even to get an approximate total.

Loss of nerve

I do believe that we are now at a historical turning point where decisions we make in respect of new technology will have a profound effect upon the manner in which our species develops. As matters now stand we are becoming increasingly dependent – some would say abjectly so – upon machines.

Rosenbrock has cautioned against this approach. In the field of computer aided design, the computer is increasingly becoming a sort of automated design manual leaving only minor choices to the design engineer. This he suggests 'seems to me to represent a loss of nerve, a loss of belief in human ability and a further unthinking application of the doctrine of the division of labour'. He further points out that the designer is thus reduced to making a series of routine choices between fixed alternatives in which case 'his skill as a designer is not used and decays' (Rosenbrock 1977).

The same underlying systems design philosophy is now evident across most areas of intellectual activity. The outcome could be an abject dependence on systems and an inability to 'think for ourselves'. However, we still have a historical window which may well be closing but which might still allow for the design of systems in a symbiotic manner to make the best use of human attributes together with those of the system.

Half a century ago the Turing Test was devised to distinguish between human beings and machines. All around the world today we see examples of humans behaving more like machines and machines more like human beings. The development is in the form of a convergence whereas what is required is one based on symbiosis.

Parody becomes reality

In the BBC comedy series Little Britain, the character Carol is a bored and indifferent bank employee. When a customer asks for a £2,000 loan she types in a few figures and declares smugly: 'Computer says no'. Becoming increasingly anxious the customer makes a number of suggestions including a smaller loan and meeting the Manager. Getting the same response the customer makes a final attempt saying 'Is there anything I can do?' Carol whispers to the computer and repeats 'computer says no'.

All of this so resonates with the public's experience that there is now a brisk market for badges, fridge magnets, key-rings and cartoons bearing the slogan 'computer says no'. You can even get a ring tone for your mobile declaring it. In the parody Carol at least speaks to the customer but the reality can be much more alarming.

When a Rochdale resident had no response whatsoever to three urgent e-mail messages to the Council's Planning Department objecting to the erection of a structure, he eventually established that the messages had been screened out by Rochdale's anti-porn software due to his inclusion of the dreaded word 'erection' (Press report 2006). The computer had said 'no' and the plans were passed before the protest could be considered as the system was devoid of the contextual understanding that a human being would have applied. Such experiences are now becoming commonplace even as IT equipment manufacturers proudly proclaim in adverts that their products help you 'Take back control'.

On your bike

The nature of technological change in its current form is that propositional knowledge becomes more significant than tacit knowledge. This results in 'know that' being more important than 'know how'.

Tacit knowledge comes from 'learning by doing' and results in the ability to judge situations based on experience. Propositional knowledge is based more on analysis and calculation. Within the human centred tradition, a symbiosis of the two and a creative interaction of them is essential. This is particularly true in the case of skilled activities.

The nature of tacit knowledge is that (to quote Polanyi): 'There are things we know but cannot tell'. In his seminal paper he continues:

> 'I can say I know how to ride a bicycle or how to swim but it does not mean that I can tell how I managed to keep my balance on a bike or keep afloat when swimming. I may not have the slightest idea of how I do this or even an entirely wrong or grossly imperfect idea of it and yet can go on cycling and swimming merrily.'

He points out that there are two kinds of knowledge which invariably enter jointly into any act of knowing a complex entity. There is firstly knowing a thing by attending to it. In that way that we attend to the entity as a whole. And secondly there is knowing a thing by relying on our awareness of its purpose of attending to an entity to which it contributes. A detailed explanation of this is given by Polanyi himself (Polanyi 1962).

Use–abuse

One of the key strands of the debate about human centred systems in the United Kingdom arose not so much in academic circles as in the industrial context of Lucas Aerospace. The company employed some 18,000 skilled craftsmen, prototype fitters, engineers, metallurgists, control systems engineers, scientists and laboratory staff. In the early seventies the company was one of the world's largest manufacturers of aerospace actuators, generators, systems and auxiliary items.

It was clear that the company was embarking on a rationalisation strategy and it eventually emerged that some 4,000 of these world class technologists were facing unemployment. Several leading members of trade unions were engaged in debates in the continuing discussion from the sixties on the role of science and technology in society. These discussions went far beyond the use/abuse model and questioned the nature of science and technology itself.

There was a vigorous discussion about the gap between the potential of science and technology and its reality. Furthermore, there was a questioning of the assumption that science – in its own terms at least – had come to monopolise the notion of the rational and could therefore be counter-posed with irrationality and suspicion. Indeed it came to be seen as a means by which irrationality could be exercised. In discussions and exchanges of correspondence with organisations such as the British

Society for Social Responsibility in Science through to academics in the United States, it gradually began to be realised that far from being neutral, science and technology actually reflected sets of values causing us to speak in terms of the control of nature, the exploitation of natural resources and the manipulation of data.

One best way?

It was clear that within science and technology there is the notion of the 'one best way'. However, viewing them as part of culture which produced different music, different literature and different artefacts, why should there not be differing forms of science and technology? Furthermore there was an increasing realisation that science and technology had embodied within it many of the assumptions of the society giving rise to it.

Space will not permit a detailed exploration of these extraordinary developments. Suffice it to say that the workforce produced a plan for what they called 'Socially Useful, Environmentally Desirable Production'. They produced and demonstrated a road/rail vehicle, prototypes of city cars and they designed and produced a range of medical products all as an alternative to structural unemployment. There were also a variety of products proposed for third world countries. In discussions dealing with how these products would be produced, it was suggested that producing these in the usual Tayloristic, alienating fashion would be unacceptable and so there arose in parallel a searching and probing discussion about the notion of human centred systems which would celebrate human skill and ingenuity rather than subordinate the human being to the machine or system.

In the discussions which led to the widely acclaimed Lucas Workers' Plan (Cooley 1991), there needed to be practical examples so that the polarised options of development could be recognised. That is, whether the process should be total automation and machine based systems or those which would build on human skill and ingenuity.

The European Economic Community sponsored a major research programme with research institutes and private companies in Denmark, Germany and the United Kingdom to produce a human centred system and the positive results of this are reported elsewhere (Cooley 1993).

Telechirics – high tech, high touch

Another practical example arose from the design need to produce a submersible vehicle capable of carrying out repairs in hazardous offshore environments. Initial considerations of a highly automated device indicated the huge computing and feedback capabilities necessary if humans were to be excluded from the process.

It was recognised that a telechiric device could work in a remote and hazardous environment but provide feedback – audio, tactile and visual to skilled operators in a safe environment. Such devices were already in use in other hazardous environments such as nuclear power. Thus telechiric devices became one of the product proposals in the Lucas Plan and emphasis was laid upon the wider application of such environments, not least in the medical field. In all cases the systems were designed such as to celebrate and enhance the skill and ability to judge of the human beings involved.

Look and feel

In the case of surgery, some of the sensationalist press headlines refer to 'robotic surgeons'. In fact the reality is that some of these systems would enhance the skill of the surgeon rather than diminish it. An example is in the field of minimal invasive surgery. These systems provide enhanced dexterity precision and control which may be applied to many surgical procedures currently performed using standard laparoscopic techniques. In fact the systems now reported succeed in providing the surgeons with all the clinical and technical capabilities of open surgery whilst enabling them to operate through tiny incisions.

As one of the companies producing such systems point out, it succeeds in maintaining the same 'look and feel' as that of open surgery. The surgeon is provided with a 'tool' to enhance and extend his or her skill whilst the patient may experience a whole range of improved outcomes, e.g. reduced trauma to the body, shorter hospital stay, less scarring and improved cosmesis. It is the judgment of the skilled surgeon that drives the system, not the technology.

Cavalier disregard

It is gratifying to see the emergence of some systems displaying many of the symbiotic attributes *AI and Society* has been espousing. Alas, the dominant tendency is still to confer life on systems whilst diminishing human involvement. Designers do so with cavalier disregard for potential human competence. Quantitative comparisons of human and systems capabilities are questionable and they do not compare like with like. However it is sobering on occasion to reflect upon the ballpark comparison. Thus Cherniak (Cherniak 1988) suggests that the massive battle management software of the Strategic Defence Initiative is 'at least a 100 times smaller than the estimated size of the mind's programme'.

Networks

Human and technology networks can encourage and stimulate people to be innovative and creative. To encourage people to think in these terms, we need a form of enterprise culture. However, universities and conventional secondary schools disregard such attributes because many are not predictable, repeatable or quantifiable. From a democratic standpoint, we need to redirect science and technology because more and more of our citizens are opposed to its present form and to those who own and control it.

A recent survey of EU citizens shows that if you ask them whom they can believe when informed about issues such as bio-engineering and genetic modification, only about 21% believe that you can accept what the multinationals tell you, which suggests to me that there are still a lot of trusting people out there. Then if you ask them what about universities, only 28% say that you can believe what the universities say because they are frequently apologists for the big companies. However, if you ask them 'Can you believe what Greenpeace tells you?' 54% will say 'Yes'.

Now this survey is a very important warning for us. If we have lost the trust of our citizens its no use pleading that they cannot or have not understood, for it is our fault for failing to communicate adequately. There are ways of communicating if we really want without making a virtue out of complexity.

Kindred spirits

Challenging the given orthodoxy is a precarious and lonely affair. It is therefore important to build up and participate in a supportive network of kindred spirits. This may take many forms, one example is the Institute Without Walls set up by *AI & Society*. The exchange of ideas and the development of collaborative projects are all important.

The support of funding bodies was likewise important with the Greater London Enterprise Board gaining European Union research funding for Esprit 1217 – to design and build and demonstrate a human centred manufacturing system. Funding was also made available by the EU FAST project – to set up a team of experts from European Union member states which would produce a report.

The ensuing report was entitled 'European Competitiveness in the Twenty-First Century: the Integration of Work, Culture and Technology'.

It was part of the FAST proposal for a research and development programme on 'Human Work in Advanced Technological Environments'. The report provided practical examples of human enhancing systems and called for an industrial and cultural renaissance. It advocated that new forms of education should facilitate the transmission of a culture valuing proactive, sensitive and creative human beings.

In 1990, the European Union commissioned and published 26 reports in its Anthropocentric Production Systems (APS) research papers series. Several of these were based on an analysis of the potential of APS for individual member states.

Cherish skill and judgment

During the formulation of the original ideas, the International Metalworkers' Federation held a conference in 1984 and hosted a presentation by the author entitled 'Technology, Unions and Human Needs'. The presentation, subsequently published as a 58 page report in 11 languages including Finnish and Japanese, was circulated to the Federation's members worldwide.

Publicity for these ideas at the more popular level was also important as it is spurious to talk about a democratic society if the public cannot influence the manner in which technology is developing. In this context, the 1-h television programme in the Channel 4 (London) Equinox series, which was presented by the author, caused considerable interest as did a number of interviews and articles in the more popular press. TV Choice London produced an educational video 'Factory of the Future' explaining the application of human centred systems which valorise human skill and judgment.

The wriggling worm

Education – like democracy – can only be partially given and for the remainder, it must be taken. Indeed, taking it is part of the process itself. Some of those designing IT systems for education behave as though a body of knowledge can be downloaded on to a human brain. It is true that some of these systems are impressive and used as a tool to aid human learning they are, and will continue to be, of great significance. The range of options, images and supporting films and graphic animation can indeed be overwhelming. However, it should be noted that in many cases they come between us and the real world. They provide us with forms of second and third order reality and information.

This may be explained by a simple example. Any child can get an impressive range of support from the internet and learning systems but this form of knowledge is very different from that acquired by one who goes into their local wood, lifts up a stone, picks up a worm and feels it wriggling in the palm of his hand. To this tactile input may then be added contextual information – summer or winter? Farms in the background? Was there the scent and feel of damp soil or decaying leaves?

So I suggest that in education, in coming years, we are going to acquire learning in developing situations where there will be the form of explicit knowledge you acquire in a university, but of equal importance will be the implicit knowledge and the informal situations that really advise our lives. It is essential to understand that if we just proceed on this mechanistic basis, the mistakes we make will be truly profound and creative opportunities will be missed.

Natural science?

We are frequently told that the best way we can proceed is within a rule-based system. This is absolutely extraordinary! As any active trade unionist knows, the way to stop anything in its tracks is to work to rule. It is all the things that we do outside the rule-based system that keeps everything going.

As matters now stand, the given scientific methodology can only accept that a procedure is scientific if it displays the three predominant characteristics of the natural sciences: predictability, repeatability and mathematical quantifiability. These by definition preclude intuition, subjective judgment, tacit knowledge, dreams, imagination, heuristics, motivation and so I could go on. So instead of calling these the natural sciences, perhaps they should be re-named the unnatural sciences. There are other ways of knowing the world than by the scientific methodology.

Furthermore, when we talk of informating people rather than automating them we need to be clear that we are talking about information and not data. Transforming data into information requires situational understanding which the human can bring to bear. This information can then be so applied as to become knowledge which in turn is absorbed into a culture and thereby becomes wisdom (Cooley 2002).

The mistress experience

Reductionists have much to answer for. They have intimidated those who proceed on the basis of tacit knowledge. Even the giants of our civilisation were derided by them.

Thus we have Leonardo's spirited riposte: 'They say that not having learning, I will not speak properly of that which I wish to elucidate. But do they not know that my subjects are to be better illustrated from experience than by yet more words? Experience, which has been the mistress of all those who wrote well and thus, as mistress, I will cite her in all cases' (Cooley 1991). The academic reductionists had even enacted a law to prevent master builders calling themselves a 'master' because it may have been confused with the academic title 'magister'.

Perfect flower of good manners

As early as the thirteenth century, Doctors of Law were moved to protest formally at these academic titles being used by practical people whose structures and designs demonstrated competence of the highest order. Thus the separation between intellectual and manual work; between theory and practice, was being further consolidated at that stage, and the title Dr Lathomorum was gradually eliminated. The world was already beginning to change at the time when the following epitaph could be written for the architect who constructed the nave and transepts of Saint Denis:

> 'Here lies Pierre de Montreuil, a perfect flower of good manners, in this life a Doctor of Stones.'

Significantly, following this period and in most of the European languages there emerged the word DESIGN or its equivalent, coincident with the need to describe the occupational activity of designing. This is not to suggest that designing was a new activity, rather it indicated that designing was to be separated from doing and tacit knowledge separated from propositional knowledge (Cooley 1991).

Liberating human imagination

Within the human centred tradition, liberating human imagination is pivotal. This is true in the hardest of the sciences as it is in music or literature. Einstein said on one occasion 'imagination is more important than knowledge'. Furthermore, when pressed to reveal how he arrived at the theory of relativity, he is said to have responded 'When I was a child of 14 I asked myself what it might be like to ride on a beam of light and look back at the world'.

In a wider sense, we need to emphasise all the splendid things that humans can do.

This is in contrast to the defect model which emphasises what they cannot do. The destructiveness of viewing humans in this manner is dramatically highlighted in the extraordinary passage in James Joyce's

Finnegans Wake when he describes the purveyors of this negative approach as:

> 'Sniffer of carrion, premature gravedigger, seeker of the nest of evil in the bosom of a good word, you, who sleep at our vigil and fast for our feast, you with your dislocated reason …' (Cooley 2005).

Confucius

This article has been wide ranging and will have raised a number of controversial issues. The references provide a framework in which to explore the ideas further. Some parts of it deal with cutting edge new technologies, yet it is gratifying to think that we can revert to Confucius to encapsulate these ideas so succinctly.

> 'I hear and I forget. I see and I remember. I do and I understand.'

References

Cherniak C (1988) *Undebuggability and cognitive science*. Commun Assoc Comput Mach 31(4):402–412

Cooley M (1991) *Architect or bee?: the human price of technology*. Chatto & Windus/The Hogarth Press, London. 2nd Impression 1991

Cooley M (1993) *Skill and competence for the 21st century*. PROC: IITD conference, Galway, April 1993

Cooley M (2002) *Stimulus points: making effective use of IT in health*. Workshop. Post Grad Department. Brighton & Sussex Medical School 14.10.2002

Cooley M (2005) *Re-Joyceing engineers*. Artif Intell Soc 19:196–198

Dreyfus HL, Dreyfus SE (1986) *Mind over machine*. The Free Press 1986

Joseph C (1999) Article, *The Times*, London 20.04.1999

Mazlish B (1967) *The fourth discontinuity*. Technol Cult 8(1):3–4

Mumford L (1963) *Technics and civilisation*. Harcourt Brace Jovanovich, New York, pp 13–15

Pearson K (1976) *Computer power and human reason* (cited in Weizenbaum J). WH Freeman & Co, San Francisco, p 25

Polanyi M (1962) *Tacit knowing: its bearing on some problems of philosophy*. Rev Mod Phys 34(4):601–616 123

AI & Soc Press report (2006) Report in *Daily Mail* 31.05.2006

Rapoport A (1963) *Technological models of the minds*. In: Sayre KM, Crosson FJ (eds) *The modelling of the mind: computers and intelligence*. The University of Notre Dame Press, pp 25–28

Rogers L (1999) Article, *Sunday Times* 18.04.1999, p 7

Rosenbrock HH (1977) *The future of control*. Automatica 13:389–392
Rosenbrock HH (1988) *Engineering as an art*. Artif Inell Soc 2:315–320
Rosenbrock HH (1990) *Machines with a purpose*. Oxford University Press, Oxford, pp 122–124. (See also Book Review in AI & Society vol 5, no.1)
Rosenbrock HH (2002) USSHER cited in '*A Gallimaufry of Quaint Conceits*'. Control Systems Centre, UMIST
Weizenbaum (1976) *Computer power and human reason*. WH Freeman & Co., San Francisco, p 25

With grateful acknowledgements to AI and Society and Springer-Verlag London Limited 2007

M. Cooley & Technology Innovation Associates, 99 Sussex Place, Slough, UK. e-mail: m.cooley@btconnect.com

Revisiting Tom Paine

Trevor Griffiths interviewed by Ann Talbot

It is three years since we published Trevor Griffiths' screenplay about the life of the eighteenth century revolutionary Thomas Paine (These are the Times, *Spokesman £15). Paine's bicentenary falls in 2009. Ann Talbot interviewed Griffiths for the World Socialist Web Site (www.wsws.org). Her remarks are in italics, and the replies in ordinary type. Her review of the screenplay in the context of Griffiths' other work appears in the Reviews section.*

It is highly unusual for a screenplay to be published, but Griffiths has taken this step because, after working on this project for over a decade, he and the producer Richard Attenborough have been unable to get financial backing. Hollywood is just not interested in a film about the life of one of the most radical and significant figures of the eighteenth century, who played a leading role in both the American and French Revolutions. Yet readings of the screenplay have attracted substantial audiences, who have been quick to recognise both the quality of Griffiths' writing and the contemporary relevance of Paine's life.

* * *

What drew you to Tom Paine?

I had a problem with Tom Paine to start with because I had a problem with the eighteenth century. I'd taken a rather stupid view that the eighteenth century was so much less interesting for anyone interested in politics than the nineteenth century.

I got a call from Dickie Attenborough in 1988 or '87, who wanted to know if I would work with him on a screenplay about Thomas Paine. And for all kinds if reasons I said: well I'm not really sure that I want to do that, and in any case I'm not free. And he said: well I can wait. Anyway, it was about nine months later when I finally got to meet with him. Somewhere still I've got a napkin, a napkin off a train, the restaurant of a train, where I wrote down everything I knew about Paine. It just about filled a napkin, one side. But at least I thought I ought to have some notes ready.

So I went down and talked with him and realised that he was asking me what to write. Hollywood doesn't do that. I mean film doesn't do that. When film comes at you it knows what it wants you to write. It may not *tell* you that it knows what it wants.

So I started re-reading Paine. I knew nothing about his life – I mean I knew that he'd been involved in the American Revolution and that he'd been involved in the French Revolution, but I didn't know much else about him.

So I started reading books about him and his political writings, and then I began to feel: well there is a film here and I'm probably well placed to write it. I think I wrote the first draft in 1990 or 1991 and the second draft in 1993 and the third draft in 1996 or 1997 and the fourth draft in 1999. And each of those drafts was a response to a particular moment in the preproduction process – trying to find producers, a distributing company, a studio if necessary, associate producers and then a kind of infrastructure of staff of arts people, company managers, all of those people and locations.

Did they want a big name to play Paine?

Yes. Well you've looked at the film and even in that version, which is a heavily chopped version, it's around four hours and the cost then would have been X million and now its probably $170 million to make that film.

Is that the blockage?

I think cost has been a huge blockage. It's just lying across the road to production like a fallen tree. It's been very difficult to get round it. To Dickie's credit he has never ever, ever suggested that we start again and make a 108 minute film.

He's very committed to it?

He knows it's a rare and extraordinary piece. It's not your average Hollywood script. It's really not. He played around for a time with two movies. Let's make two movies and we show them on separate nights. But no one was interested in that in Hollywood and no one was really interested in the eighteenth century.

You've given Paine more humanity than I've ever seen in a biography of him.

I still haven't got to the root of Paine because he's a difficult guy. I've always found him contentious and awkward and fractious, difficult to get hold of, constantly slipping out of your intellectual understanding. Like Strindberg in a way. Like people from another age. Totally, exhaustingly, obsessed by the whole tree of knowledge. He was incredible. He had real feelings. He spent a lot of time reading, a lot of time writing, a lot of time walking, a lot of time with experiments with gases in ponds. All of those are scenes – not in my head – they're on the page. But they've all gone. There's a limit to what you can do.

You've given him more personal relationships than the historians allow him.

It would have been unthinkable to do a piece about anybody that didn't involve some aspect of their humanity, which is usually expressed in relational terms. There are a number of key relationships. A key relationship is with the black kid Will. Another key relationship is with Lotte, the daughter of the landlady, Marthe.

The relationship with Jefferson is also much warmer than is generally acknowledged. I mean Paine suffered, the longer he lived the more he suffered from neglect and malignity. People wanted to suppress him. They wanted to put those important books down once and for all. It started with the British government – the Pitt government – sorting out a biographer – a fake biographer who was a spy – to rubbish him. So that first so-called marriage and the second one became evidence of Paine's brutality, bestiality, and lack of responsibility, inhuman arrogant behaviour.

It's not difficult to demonstrate that was rubbish. But thinking and imagining him in relationships for which there is no evidential provenance, or scarcely any, or just hints and whispers, that was the task of the writer. And there are some footnotes in books about the landlady and the way that his associates in Philadelphia talked about him. They wrote letters to each other. In his correspondence with Jefferson, John Adams refers to the indignity that was done to the landlady by Paine staying there on his own, and taking dinner with her and her daughter, and behaving familiarly with her when people were round at the house. We understand the custom and practice of eighteenth century people of that class, and there would be that slight alarm about the unconventionality of Paine's position there. It spoke to me very clearly of a man who was very lonely and was, in fact, sharing a bed and a life with a woman he really respected, so that's what I wrote.

The second one is a different kind of rumour. Carnet, I call her Carnet, Madame de Bonneville,[1] she was very close with him, no question, but so was the husband. She did have three kids, one of whom she called Thomas Paine de Bonneville. The first one she called Benjamin, after Benjamin Franklin.

But we can't suspect anything there, surely?

Well I do, because Franklin fucked everything that moved, especially in France. The King of France, this is true, the King of France had several mistresses for whom he had Sèvres piss pots made, piss pots with an image of Ben Franklin painted at the bottom, because he was such a lecher. Everywhere he went his hands stuck on somebody. I love Franklin. I think he's ace. But that was his life anyway and he spent a lot of time away from home. I think he was the guy who got all the cogs working at the right time, and that's how that revolution somehow clicked into gear.

Franklin had the contacts in England among people who knew Paine, didn't he?

Absolutely, and for 30 years he was, not secretly, but he was just quietly bringing likely lads into America and placing them in positions where they might be useful. You get the sense, for example, that Matlack, Cannon[2] and various other people who became part of that network of revolutionaries in Pennsylvania had been put there in some previous moment – in some previous decade – to be useful when they were needed – when caucuses were afoot and all the rest of it. I love, suddenly I'm in love with that period, as soon as I write it and appropriate parts of it then it becomes important to me.

I've never seen the eighteenth century so real and tangible. How did you achieve that?

It's hard to say this. It's the most abandoned piece of historical writing I've done. I sought within my own principles, and my own craft, to validate and justify every major decision about what that century shall look and smell like to the person watching the film or reading the text, and I've gone to great lengths to find out those things I didn't know. I wrote a play which you ought to read – it's called *Who shall be Happy?* It's about Danton on the final night of his life. I had the cast of that play read *Perfume*, the novel. That's about the sense of smell. It's a murder story, but it's just loaded with what it was like to be alive in the eighteenth century. Your nose led you to places, not your eyes, because everything looked fairly similar – grey and dirty – but your nose would tell you where the bread shop was or where the hostelry was. So I had them working for a day, just the two of them with blindfolds on, just smelling each other. It sounds crazy, but it really worked.

Why do you think Paine's interesting now?

Why do I think Paine's interesting now? It's very difficult to find where the purchase of Marx is in the contemporary political world. You don't find it. It's kind of been sidelined. The Marxist approach has been blocked. When the Soviet Union collapsed I immediately went back to the previous revolution, the French Revolution, and began to say: well, if I can't solve the problems of the world via the Russian Revolution I'll have a look at the French Revolution, because I know it had a huge agenda and only a fragment of that agenda was ever realized in historical terms. So I began to examine that, and one of the things that came out of that was the Danton play, which, at another level, was a literary riposte to a great Buchner play *Danton's Death*,[3] which I think is a great play, but one that somehow romanticizes what Danton was up to.

So I looked at the French Revolution and said: well, let's see what's unfinished and finish it, at least at the level of literature and drama. Which took me, interestingly, back into Tom Paine, because I thought: I've finished Tom Paine, it isn't going to be done; there is nothing to be done. Screenplays are like snow on grass. It needs a bit of heat and they're gone. You never see them again. And I reached out for something with *These are the Times*. I reached out to have it printed if it was not going to be recorded on film. If it was not going to be played, realized and given a chance to live in people's minds and hearts and practices, then I would at least enable it to go in individually to people as a read.

First of all you've got to apply for permission to do that. You don't own it. A Hollywood producer is the only person who's allowed to have his or her name associated in the Library of Congress with your book, with your script. It's not *These are the Times* by Trevor Griffiths, its *These are the Times* by whoever was the producer. I know it's astonishing. We don't know how feudally we live. We really don't. But we're talking about Tom Paine.

Yes, Tom Paine. At the end of the screenplay his grave is still open and we hear his words about the need for a revolution. Then it cuts to the present and we see modern New York and he's still talking about the need for a revolution. Is that what would draw people back again and again to see it?

Yes, rich and poor chained together. I first read that in public in Toronto. I'd just written it that year and there were people crying afterwards who came up and asked me to sign it.

We've sold I don't know how many books, maybe 1,500, maybe 2,000, which at £15 a shot, and a book that you cannot get reviewed, is not bad.

You cannot get it reviewed because no one reviews screenplays, because screenplays are not published, really. They are, but it's such a sliver of interest in the literary world.

Within all of this there is a craft trajectory of which I'm always aware. I've written about five or six screenplays and they're all very specific screenplays. But I think this is the best screenplay I've written. I think it's good. It's a very exciting piece of work.

It's very contemporary.

I think it is. It's become increasingly, and this is the worrying thing, it's become almost autobiographical. In the 12 years I was writing it, in those different drafts, more of myself was going into it. It's interesting that you talk about Paine, as he's historically presented, as being extremely lonely, because I think there is loneliness in that life, and it's a loneliness I associate with my own life, which is not a loneliness about not having people to love, and to trust, and to cherish and treasure, but also just about the craft of writing. Lonely is too emotional a word, but you do it on your own.

I'm keen on group writing. The very first we ever did was called *Lay By*. I mean that was Brenton and Hare and Poliakoff[4] and me. It was one wet Sunday afternoon when we were supposed to have a meeting about politics in the theatre. It was pouring down and we were all fed up. So we said instead of doing that meeting why don't we write a play. And we got a role of lining paper and some pens and started writing a play which went on to Edinburgh and became the darling of the festival. People were fainting it was so exciting. It disappeared without trace thereafter.

That's quite a group.

It was an interesting group. I always knew it would be a very limited time that we were allowed to work like that. Because it's not the nature of capitalism to have people licensed to knock shit out of it at every opportunity. They don't mind as long as we're ineffectual. But if we start getting a voice in things, and helping people to side against what capital wants, then we're in trouble. In 1979 I did an interview and said that we're going to see a lot of people, whom we now absolutely trust as a comrade, ducking behind doors when they see you. What I meant to say was, and what I think I did say, was that as it gets tougher to make a living we're going to see people breaking, buckling and doing what's required of them. And I think on the whole that's true.

Do you think a young writer now could do what you did then?

No. No, I mean the trajectory is completely different. You can't have politics in your bag. You just can't. It's not allowed. It's not only not allowed, it's found to be quite distasteful.

I didn't invent myself. The world invented me. I came out of teaching. I came out of New Left Clubs. I came out of the Campaign for Nuclear Disarmament and the Committee of 100. I had an active back history pushing me forward. So when I got to confronting producers and production units and the BBC and all of that stuff, I didn't feel that I was on my own. I felt that I was shoulder to shoulder with a hell of a lot of people.

When did that period end?

[laughing] That was 1997 and I was the last one to be killed. You keep having to shout from the grave.

In the Paine screenplay and also in The Party *there's the same line that you're only dead if you don't take root in other people. Do you think that's a very important concept for you?*

Yes, I do because we all have other people in us. I could start listing mine. There's huge numbers of people. People you've met. People you've read. I never met Kurt Vonnegut, but I could tell you about his books and the way they've lodged in me. And how they've kept me going since. So, yes, people and books. And books are people, but with pages.

Footnotes:

1 Mme Marguerite Bonneville see: John Keane, *Tom Paine: A Political Life* (London: Bloomsbury, 1995) for the rumours about her connection with Paine.

2 Timothy Matlack (1736-1829) and James Cannon (1740-1782) were key figures among the supporters of independence in Philadelphia. See: http://www.archives.upenn.edu/histy/features/1700s/people

3 Georg Büchner German playwright (1813-1837)

4 Howard Brenton (1942-) English playwright and screenwriter; Sir David Hare (1947-) English playwright; Stephen Poliakoff (1952-) English playwright, screenwriter and director.

Reviews

Eat, Drink and Make Merry?

Paul Roberts, *The End of Food: The Coming Crisis in the World Food Industry*, Bloomsbury, 416 pages, ISBN 9780747588818, £12.99

The author of *The End of Oil* has now written an equally well researched study of what he quite properly calls 'the Food Industry'. For that is what the mass production of cheap food has become, but cannot be continued much longer for several reasons. The first is that large scale production of grains in the main producing areas – North America, Argentina, Australia – needs great quantities of water, and we are using up the supplies, and that is even before climate change reduces them. The second is that more and more grain is being used to increase meat production to meet demand in the newly rich populations of Asia, and now also to provide bio-fuel to replace failing oil and gas. The third is the very failing reserves of oil and gas, which provide the base of the food industry, its mechanisation, transport and the raw material for its fertilisers and pesticides. The fourth, which already worries some people most, is the growing danger of pandemic disease – with possible destruction of all fowls and much livestock – following from concentrated animal production and inadequate inspection.

This is a pretty alarming list of problems for which answers are simply not apparent. The evidence for each of the four problems is rigorously examined by the author. What he believes to be fundamentally wrong with the whole current food system is that the demand for production of the greatest possible quantity at the lowest possible cost has involved larger and larger scale, until a very small number of giant corporations own or control global output. This is to be found in the sale of seeds, the growing of crops, rearing of cattle and hogs, shepherding, battery chicken farming, and the processing, transporting and retailing of the final produce. At each stage just two or three giant companies dominate the world market, and to keep lowering costs they must keep expanding sales. Huge resources of energy and chemicals are consumed beyond what is sustainable, and at the same time vast quantities go to waste. Despite rigid controls, pandemics can easily occur.

The conclusions from this analysis are pretty clear. To survive, the human race will need very soon to adopt a totally different way of feeding ourselves, and an end to the present global system. Paul Roberts quotes the Cuban success in refashioning its food production on a sustainable model, as one experiment forced upon the Cubans by the cutting off of Soviet oil supplies and the boycott of Cuban trade with the US. This experiment could show the way to produce food without oil, fertilisers and pesticides. But Roberts warns that Cuba is still short of meat and dairy products, and had special advantages of a warm, wet climate, large reserves of labour, and an authoritarian political regime that all helped to make such a major change possible. An increase of vegetable growing and of small live stock in gardens and allotments is already taking place in the United States and in the United Kingdom and elsewhere, but the scale is still minute in relation to what is needed.

Paul Roberts proposes as an essential first step state intervention to end the globalisation of food production and to require that it be regionalised. This would at least reduce transport costs and the spread of epidemics, and Roberts argues that it would be more climate friendly and energy efficient. But he does not believe that the spread of markets retailing the produce of small farmers is a practical solution either from the point of view of cost or of food safety. The problem of a world food system that results in one fifth of the world's people starving, while at the other extreme roughly the same number are dying of obesity, requires radical new thinking. To replace the meat industry, Roberts puts much faith in the development of aquaculture, and especially the latest forms of open water production which create less pollution and generate less disease than current fish farming. Fish convert feed into protein far more efficiently than land animals.

Some such minimal solutions may be adopted, but the will to make a fundamental change in the now firmly established habits of eating convenience foods is lacking, even more than the determination to use less energy and create less CO2. The attractions of a return to home cooking, gardening and convivial family meals seem not to be strong enough to change our way of living. Perhaps Roberts is right, that only hunger and cold, from lack of food and power, will force us to make a better world. In the mean time we eat, drink and make merry.

Michael Barratt Brown

South America Ahoy!

Tariq Ali, *Pirates of the Caribbean – Axis of Hope* (revised edition), Verso, 308 pages, paperback ISBN 9781844672486, £8.99

Tariq Ali has been an ever-present figure on the British and international

Left for more years than the reviewer cares to remember, and always an inspirational figure battling against the odds on a wide variety of issues. Activist, writer, broadcaster, a true socialist polymath, he might be getting ready to draw his pension, but as this text makes clear, he has lost none of his hopes for a truly radical break with the current global dispensation. Neither has his ageing inclined him to join the ranks of those he describes as '"matured" and crumbled or, to put it bluntly, sold out'.

In fact the first chapter, 'The Age of Disinformation', deals with the 'mass conversion' triggered by the collapse of Soviet 'socialism' and the consequent rallying of erstwhile former friends of the Left around the banner of the Washington Consensus and the 'neo-liberal free market'. In what might be termed a spirited 'piratical' defence, Ali cuts a swathe through the underpinnings of the Washington Consensus and their hirelings within the Western media who seek to isolate, undermine and misrepresent the evolving radical movements of the South American continent, rendering Venezuela and Bolivia in particular to the pariah status so successfully foisted onto Cuba, in the popular captive Western mind-set. Lambasting the BBC and ABC as the 'disinformation corporations', and singling out *The Economist* and the *Financial Times* for their predictably biased treatment of the coup to unseat Chávez, he has some deservedly harsh words indeed for the community of 'reptilian journalists' concerned. Also mentioned in dispatches is Denis MacShane, Labour MP for Rotherham and former Minister for Europe no less, who worries that 'Tony Blair is very disturbed about the turn to the Left in Latin America' and categorises Chávez as a 'ranting demagogue'. The French media fare little better, *Le Monde* and *Libération* being particularly sad cases whose coverage, the author maintains, did undoubtedly deteriorate after 11 September 2001, taking an avowedly 'Atlanticist posture'. This is an exhilarating and stimulating chapter, which not only trounces the detractors but demonstrates the efficacy and need for books such as this to redress the information deficit.

After this rousing introductory chapter the rest of the book broadly maps out the current picture, within a concise historical outline, of Venezuelan, Bolivian and Cuban politics, situating the analysis in the overall context of South American and global politics; a fairly tall order even for a book of 300 pages, but one which the author manages to accomplish with both panache and insight. Ali shows a clear grasp of the differences between these radicalised nations, and how their differing historical experiences have influenced the forms their struggles have adopted. The ramifications of Cuba's guerrilla war of liberation and subsequent US blockade contrasts with the parliamentary constitutional gaining of power by the Left in Bolivia and Venezuela. In contrast, however, many threads tie them together: the role of the military; the participation of the indigenous population in the struggle for economic and social liberation; the problems of structural racism. Differences there may be, but there is always one common denominator. The main shared stumbling block to any continental advance is the opposition of the United States and its allies, and herein lies the primary purpose of this book: to undermine the Washington Consensus and its hold over public opinion and to provide a vehicle of support for these radical movements. This is not to say that the book shies away from mentioning difficulties, past and present, particularly with regard to Cuba. One the other hand, Ali finds the Workers Party administration in Brazil a great disappointment and scathingly refers to President Lula da Silva as the 'tropical Tony Blair', with good reason. Also discussed, albeit briefly, is the attempt by the Kirchner administration in Argentina to find a middle course between, as the book puts it, 'a third way between Chávez and Lula'.

The book contains some interesting passages on the life and times of Simon Bolivar and his importance for a new generation of South American revolutionaries. Bolivar, dismissed by Marx, as that 'dastardly, most miserable and meanest of blackguards' was a colourful yet determined revolutionary whose privileged upbringing allowed an education in the new radicalism sweeping Europe in the late 18th century. These ideas combined with his observations of the reality of colonial life in South America caused him to become the accomplished political and military leader so revered by today's South American revolutionaries. He died in relative obscurity, a disappointed and resentful man, having been sidelined by the more grasping of his military colleagues, but still willing to fight on to end colonialism. In addition, Bolivar's failure to effectively confront slavery, in spite of the support he received from the Black revolutionaries of Haiti, was, as the book makes clear, a 'tragic weakness'. One perhaps Marx had in mind?

As this is an updated revision of an earlier book it takes us up to the failed referendum of 2007 in Venezuela, and makes a number of observations regarding this. Firstly, too many issues were lumped together, and no provision was made to record the vote, reform by reform. As a result many issues, where there was probably a majority, were rejected, a valid point in the context of such a small margin for rejection overall. Secondly, the campaign was rushed, which has been accepted by many commentators and Chávez himself, but in addition Ali makes the point that if the individual proposals of the referendum had been discussed on a proposal by proposal basis it would have forced the Chavistas to campaign on a more effective 'grassroots' basis.

The book concludes with extensive appendices containing the relatively recent speech of Chávez at the UN and the speech by Evo Morales, 'Power to the People', as well as an interview with a former military colleague of Chávez. The latter is fascinating, encompassing as it does the abortive Chávez coup of 1992 and the abortive anti-Chávez coup of 2002, retold by an actual participant, Luis Reyes Reyes (a former military officer, now a state governor). In general, this book is an invigorating introduction to the new politics of South America and, as Ali himself states, it is 'not a Cuban style revolution, but a form of radical social democracy that is today unacceptable to the Washington Consensus'. No book can hope to keep pace with the twists and turns of political developments in the region, but reading this book will help to explain the undoubted difficulties and contradictions that the radical movements in South America have already confronted, and will have to confront, as well inspiring optimism for change.

John Daniels

Illegal Invasion

Gwynne Dyer, *After Iraq: Where Next for the Middle East?*, Yale University Press, 272 pages, hardback ISBN 9780300137354, £16.99

If some of the British public are confused about Middle East affairs it could be because the BBC is also confused as to its role in reporting the war in Iraq. The BBC is reluctant to mention in all its reports on Iraq that the invasion was illegal. Since the BBC lost its Chairman of Governors and its Director General for reporting, accurately, that the intelligence on Iraq's non-existent weapons of mass destruction was being manipulated into a catalogue of lies, it is hardly surprising that some of those who remain in the BBC now report the war as one deserving of public support. But that provides only false comfort for the bereaved relatives and friends of those killed, and it will lead to another generation of misled young people.

Gwynne Dyer's readable, up-to-date and well researched book provides an intelligible survey of Middle East affairs. He was Senior Lecturer in Middle Eastern and Military Studies at the Royal Military Academy,

Sandhurst, before becoming a freelance analyst and writer with a twice weekly column published in 175 newspapers in 45 countries. Here is a sample of his writing, and his probing style.

> 'In January 2002, the month after the last resistance in Afghanistan had been quelled, Bush devoted his State of the Union speech to telling the American public about his discovery of the "axis of evil", and by the end of that speech it was quite clear that the United States was going to invade Iraq. Having cheated the Islamists of an easy success in Afghanistan, Bush gave them a free kick, for the invasion of Iraq was everything that bin Laden had hoped the invasion of Afghanistan would be: 130,000 young US soldiers fighting their way through a landscape filled with terrified civilians, calling on the enormous firepower available to them whenever there seemed to be a problem, and then a prolonged, in-your-face military occupation in which Americans with little knowledge of the country and none of the language ran everything – and ran it very badly. No wonder it blew up in their faces, and began producing a steady stream of images, from Abu Ghraib to Fallujah, that horrified Muslims everywhere. Bin Laden had no way of foreseeing the American invasion of Iraq, but it certainly has produced the radicalisation of opinion in the Arab world that he had been hoping for.'

The Nuremburg trials of alleged war criminals after World War Two established the principle for the United Nations Organisation that an unprovoked attack on one country by another was a crime in international law. Let us hope that our news media make no mistake either that an occupation to govern without consent is the ultimate in human rights abuses, subsuming all others. No surprise then that the Attorney General, Lord Goldsmith, the Secretary General of the UN, General Sir Michael Rose, the Rt. Hon. E W Thomas and many other jurists, the Archbishop of Canterbury, and over one million protesters in the UK alone took the view that the invasion of Iraq without the authority of the UN was illegal. Now there are similar concerns about a threatened attack on Iran – another country with a large proportion of the world's oil reserves.

Dyer's appraisal of the consequences of an attack on Iran by the United States or by Israel is remarkably close to that offered more recently by Mohamed ElBaradei, Director General of the UN's International Atomic Energy Agency, whose inspectors have so far found no evidence of manufacture of a nuclear weapon there. ElBaradei predicted 'a ball of fire' not confined to the Middle East. Dyer wrote many pages describing several possible severe scenarios, but with one firm conclusion: most Middle East states supportive of an American presence in the Middle East would be under much pressure to cause them to leave.

When I was ten years old, in 1939, I knew about Hitler's plan to attack Poland because my teacher, who was also the headmaster, explained the news over a map of Europe every week. Mr Ramsbottom, for that was his name, of Moss Street Council School, Blackburn, communicated his dread of war even though it was not yet a fact. When I talk to 12 year old pupils and 17 year old students about human rights and the 'War on Terror' as a representative of Amnesty International, I am surprised to find that they know very little about the wars in Iraq and Afghanistan. In a class of 12 year old pupils only one, a boy, knew that Britain was at war, and that the country was Iraq. There must be few teachers like Mr Ramsbottom ready to discuss current affairs routinely with their pupils, and not enough parents to encourage them to take an interest. The 17 year old students were only slightly better informed. They had concerns about the war on terror out of all proportion to the terror that has been wrought by governments. A few thought that restoring the death penalty might help.

Dyer has no illusions about the error and futility of the war in Iraq, and the damage done not only to the people and infrastructure of Iraq – probably by now one million dead and two million refugees – but also to international law and to the United Nations. His estimates of the dangers to world peace of the threatened attacks by George W Bush and Israel on Iran need to be appraised by a larger population of parents and teachers. His speculations are well founded on the recent history of Western involvement in the countries surrounding Iraq, which he examines in the early part of the book. The speculations will be particularly useful to those criminally responsible for the illegal invasion of 2003 who remain in power – perhaps only briefly – but who still have the opportunity to effect radical changes in policy to bring about reconstruction and perhaps even peace.

Christopher Gifford

A Script for Freedom

***These are the Times: A Life of Thomas Paine*, a screenplay by Trevor Griffiths, Spokesman Books, 210 pages, ISBN 9780851246956, £15**

Screenplays are not often published; they are even less often reviewed. A film is so much the product of a collective effort that a screenplay is regarded as being in some way incomplete until it has been filmed, and yet if the same principle were applied to a play it would seem patently absurd.

No one suggests that a play cannot be discussed except in the form of a specific production. We understand the relationship between the screenplay and the film differently because of the vast corporate machinery that is required to make and distribute a film. The writer is dwarfed and seems to be an almost subsidiary figure to the director. But the distinction between screen and stage has no artistic foundation. That becomes clear when we have the opportunity to read a screenplay of the calibre of Trevor Griffiths' *These are the Times*. This is a work that stands in its own right as a piece of literature.

Griffiths is perhaps best known for having co-written the film *Reds* (1981) with Warren Beatty. That film told the story of the American revolutionary John Reed who visited the Soviet Union and wrote *Ten Days that Shook the World*, an account of the Russian Revolution. Griffiths was nominated for an Oscar for that screenplay and won a Writers Guild of America Award.

Revolution has been a major theme in all of Griffiths' work for cinema, television and the theatre. His play *Occupations* dealt with Antonio Gramsci's role in the Turin factory occupations of 1920. *The Party* was concerned with the Paris events of 1968 and the reaction to them of a group of intellectuals, writers and artists who encounter the leader of a revolutionary party. It was drawn from life and reflected Griffiths' own experience in that period. The figure of John Tagg, the revolutionary, was based on Gerry Healy, leader of the Socialist Labour League, then the British section of the International Committee of the Fourth International. *Absolute Beginners* dramatised the Bolshevik/Menshevik split in the Russian Social Democratic Party. *All Good Men* concerned the conflict between parliamentary reformism and revolutionary politics that is expressed in the relationship between a Labour Member of Parliament and his son. It was broadcast during the three-day week that the Conservative Government of Edward Heath imposed as it clashed with the miners.

Griffiths' work has been informed and shaped by the political experiences of the working class in Britain. He was born in Manchester in 1935. His father worked in the chemical industry. Griffiths was one of the first generation of working class youth to benefit from the 1944 Education Act. He went to Manchester University where he studied English. He was part of a group of new writers including David Mercer, Ken Loach, Jim Allen and Dennis Potter who were associated with Tony Garnett, who brought a new realism to British television in the 1960s. In the theatre, where much of his work has been done, he is one of a group of politicized playwrights that includes David Hare, Howard Brenton and David Edgar.

Yet Griffiths is a distinctive voice among his contemporaries. Whereas many of them seem to want to express a sense of disillusionment, Griffiths resists that prevalent intellectual trend. His writing is never cynical. That is surprising because the disillusionment has a real social basis in the position of intellectuals in capitalist society.

In *The Party*, John Tagg says to the intellectuals gathered at the house of Joe Shawcross: 'In 1919 London dockers went on strike and refused to load munitions for the White armies fighting against the Russian revolution. In 1944 dockers in Amsterdam refused to help the Nazis transport Jews to concentration camps. What can *you* do? You can't strike and refuse to handle American cargoes until they get out of Vietnam. You're outside the productive process. You have only the word. And you cannot make it become the deed. And because the people who have the power seem uneager to use it, you develop this … cynicism … this contempt.'

Griffiths' strength is that he knows what the word can and cannot do. He is aware of the limitations of words, but he has respect for his own craft as a writer. Paine is in many ways the ideal subject for him because Paine was a man of words. He was not like Washington a soldier, or like Jefferson a statesman, although he shared with both an interest in science, and he was certainly not a businessman like Morris. His power lay in his words and their ability to give expression to, and to influence the development of, social consciousness in a revolutionary period. His greatness lay in his willingness to carry on doing that in a period when the revolutionary impetus was temporarily spent.

In another respect, too, Paine is the ideal subject for Griffiths. Paine was an Englishman who became a citizen of France and of America. He regarded himself as a citizen of the world. Griffiths differs from many of the representatives of his generation of socialist-minded writers in that he has never been parochial in his outlook, either in a literary or a political sense.

Even when dealing with what might be thought of as British themes, his work has always taken in a wider horizon. His *Country*, which was a BBC *Play for Today*, is set in 1945 on the eve of the election that was to bring the Labour Party to power. It featured an English upper class family who find the stables of their country home invaded by homeless people. Within the space of a short and beautifully crafted piece, Griffiths shows how the British political élite adapted to the threat that the working class posed to them and their way of life.

In many ways *Country* is a quintessentially English piece. That character is emphasised by the way in which it was filmed. It could almost be any one of the nostalgic costume dramas in which British television excels. But Griffiths' portrayal of the English upper class was influenced by his earlier adaptation of Chekhov's *The Cherry Orchard*. His upper class characters have a depth and pathos that takes the drama to the level of serious art and gives to the class struggle in which they are involved an immediacy and intensity that is deeply disturbing. This is not a comfortable evening's entertainment. The viewer will never take the tour of an English stately home in quite the same way again. Nor will they view post-war British history in quite the same way again. Griffiths reveals the current of class struggle that runs just below the complacent surface of the parliamentary democracy that has dominated the public face of post-war political life.

A great deal of Griffiths' work for television is now almost unobtainable. His *Bill Brand* (1976), a Thames Television series about a left-wing Labour MP, and his *Food for Ravens* (BBC 1997), which was about Aneurin Bevan and the foundation of the National Health Service, seem to have vanished. The BBC commissioned *Food for Ravens* to commemorate the 100th anniversary of Bevan's birth, but then refused to network it and restricted it to a late night slot on BBC Wales.

His reputation has been a victim of the continuing rightward trajectory of British politics. Griffiths' kind of political drama is generally regarded as outmoded. There could be no greater contrast with the late 1960s and mid 1970s. Griffiths' reputation was then at its zenith. When *The Party* was first performed by the National Theatre at the Old Vic in 1973, Sir Laurence Olivier played the part of John Tagg the Glaswegian Trotskyist. It played to packed houses and brought Griffiths enthusiastic offers from television.

What the Tom Paine screenplay demonstrates is that even in the present period of eclipse Griffiths' focus on the guiding themes of his art has not lessened and his powers as a writer have, if anything, sharpened. The screenplay is a remarkable piece of work. Griffiths has always had the ability that a great portrait painter has to get inside the mind of his subject and present the inner essence of that character on the page. In *The Party* we see a revolutionary leader drawn to the very life. In *These are the Times* we have the real, living, breathing Tom Paine before us. Paine comes off the page and challenges us.

Paine emerges in a way that no history book or biography has ever presented him. That is no easy task because he was a difficult man, at war with the times that produced him; one of the finest products of his times and yet one of the most reviled. It was not easy for his contemporaries to comprehend Paine's restless character and it is not easy for us to place him. He remains a revolutionary whether in the eighteenth century or the twenty-first. For Paine the revolution did not end when the British quit America, and if he walked in on us today it would not have ended now. His project was world revolution. The injustices and the inequalities that he condemned in the eighteenth century are still with us today and Griffiths' screenplay makes an explicit connection between then and now.

In the final scene of the film, Paine's grave lies open and we hear him reading his words from *Agrarian Justice*. 'The contrast of affluence and wretchedness, continually meeting and offending the eye is like dead and living bodies chained together …' Griffiths' directions run: 'The shot tilts suddenly, reveals a modern highway, heavy with traffic, ripping past New Rochelle. Mixes with the south bound flow, to today's New York City and its images of wretchedness and affluence …'

Paine's voice continues reading: '… The great mass of the poor are become an hereditary race, and it is next to impossible for them to get out of that state of themselves … The condition of millions in every country … is now far worse than if they had been born before civilisation began …'

The shot returns to the open grave and Paine calls for a 'revolution in the state of civilization.'

In this immensely economical scene, Griffiths has summed up both Paine's revolutionary project and its relevance for today without being in the least didactic. In a matter of a few hundred words that would perhaps make a few minutes of film he has succeeded in creating a self-expanding concept that opens up to fill our minds. We see far more than he presents.

Is there some deception here? We are so accustomed to being manipulated in the cinema it is impossible not to ask. It is surely part of the stock in trade of any competent Hollywood screenwriter to know their way round the levers of human perception. Most use their knowledge in a cynical way. The better ones use it to entertain us. But Griffiths is doing more than even the best of the better screenwriters. Just as he writes characters that are fully human by portraying the essence of their souls, so he allows his audience to be fully human by appealing to what is essential in their social being. Someone coming out of this film would know more about Tom Paine for sure, but they would also know more about themselves.

It is possible that in the present political climate this film will never be made, but it is far more likely that there will come a moment when it has to be made because it will so closely express the consciousness of masses of people. In the meantime, buy the screenplay.

Ann Talbot

The Capitalist Frankenstein

Francis Wheen, *Marx's Das Kapital* : *A Biography* , Atlantic Books, 128 pages, ISBN 9781843544012, £7.99

Marx's *Das Kapital* is frequently dismissed as unreadable because of the difficult discussion of commodities in the very first chapter, and unusable because of the manifest failure of his prophesy that capitalism would be supplanted by socialism. But as Francis Wheen, who wrote one of the best full length biographies of Marx, explains in this brilliant little short biography: 'Marx's errors or unfulfilled prophecies about capitalism are eclipsed and transcended by the piercing accuracy with which he revealed the nature of the beast'. And it was as a *Frankenstein* monster that he saw capitalism, one that would destroy its own creator.

The demise of capitalism, which Marx expected, did not come in his lifetime, but within 75 years of his death, half the world – from Albania to Zimbabwe – albeit for a short time, lived under regimes that had rejected the rule of capital in favour of some form of socialism. The book, however, as Wheen argues most cogently, should not be read as prophecy or prescription, but for its analysis of the workings of the capitalist system. It continues to generate inequality, as Marx noted, not only inside even the richest countries, but also between countries on a world-wide scale. The productivity of labour is steadily increased, all forms of consumer goods are more widely available – cars, air travel, washing machines, television, mobile phones — but rather than increasing leisure time for the workers, hours are longer ('the average British employee' as Wheen quotes, 'now puts in 80,224 hours over his or her working life, as against 69,000 hours in 1981').

Far from being ended, exploitation of the workers, that is the proportion of the value of what they produce which is taken off them by the capitalist, increases all the time, 'whether their wage be high or low', as Marx insisted. In 1998, as Wheen records, 'meltdown in Russia, currency collapse in Asia and market panic around the world prompted the *Financial Times* (not a socialist paper) to wonder if we had moved from the triumph of global capitalism to its crisis in barely a decade'. The banking crisis of 2007-8 must raise the question more insistently. We should not expect the system shortly to collapse, but we should recognise how right Marx was to reveal the fundamental weakness of a system marked by capital accumulation at one pole and declining real income of workers at the other.

What, above all, Wheen makes clear about Marx's *Das Kapital* is the immense richness of allusion and illustration in the writing. Marx was never satisfied that he had got the picture quite right – and delayed publication of Volume One for many years and left the later volumes for his friend, Frederick Engels, to reconstruct from a mass of notes and drafts. It is this richness, drawn from Marx's voluminous reading in English classical literature and in official publications, that makes it so rewarding to go back to reading what he wrote 150 years ago. And the wealth of language will not disappoint. Just listen to Marx extolling the contribution of capitalists to human development as well as their threat to our humanity:

> 'The bourgeoisie, wherever it has got the upper hand, has put an end to all feudal, patriarchal, idyllic relations. It has pitilessly torn asunder the motley feudal ties that bound man to his "natural superiors", and has left remaining no other nexus between man and man than naked self-interest, than callous "cash payment". It has drowned the most heavenly ecstasies of religious fervour, of chivalrous enthusiasm, of philistine sentimentalism in the icy water of egotistical calculation. It has resolved personal worth into exchange value ...'

How could we not recognise that today?

Michael Barratt Brown

Roll up! Roll up!

Sara Gruen, *Water for Elephants*, Hodder & Stoughton, 418 pages, paperback ISBN 9780340962725, £7.99

The posters are going up all over town. They are adorned with beautiful white horses, flying trapeze artists, the jolly man in his black top hat and red tails, a lion or two, and the familiar face with the make-up and a red nose. A circus is coming to town, bringing with it untold joy for the spectators who watch the big top being erected. Behind the scenes the less familiar faces of the circus work hard to make the illusion possible, and the performers' graceful actions make it all seem so very simple to fly through the air. Similarly, Sara Gruen's beautiful writing makes it seem so easy to create a wonderful work of fiction.

Water for Elephants takes the reader back stage with access to all areas. The narrator, Jacob Jankowski, takes a look back at his life in the circus, and what a life it turns out to be. It is the 1930s and the depression has hit America hard, and the death of his parents has hit Jacob harder still. Before he is to sit his final veterinary exams at Cornell, he learns that he is orphaned and penniless. His head is reeling with this news as he makes his way into the wilderness. After a long walk in no particular direction, a train comes thundering towards him, he runs to catch one of the many cars, and lunges himself onto it and into a life beyond his wildest expectations.

This imaginary tale of one man's life in the circus combines romance with horror. Sara Gruen's narrative style reflects the 'CHUNK-a-chunk-a-chunk-a-chunk' of the train that transports Jacob around America. The tempo is quick, and every detail of this amazing journey fills the readers senses, making you cry out for more. A fabulous read that lingers long after it's finished, a bit like the circus itself.

Abi Rhodes